THE WAITING GAME

YOUTH FORUM SERIES

A YOUTH FORUM BOOK

THE WAITING GAME

by

Roy W. Fairchild

THOMAS NELSON INC.
New York / Camden

For
Jan, Nancy, and Christie

Foreword

This book is one of a series in a unique publishing effort in which Youth Research Center, Inc., Minneapolis, Minnesota, has joined with Thomas Nelson Inc., Camden, New Jersey. The books are based on the very real concerns, problems, aspirations, searchings and goals of young people today as measured by nation-wide surveys being conducted continuously by the research center.

Central to the series is the belief that we all have a compelling need to turn to a core of faith for guidelines in coping with the world in which we live. Each book deals with a specific need or concern of young people viewed in relation to the Christian faith. By drawing upon the results of the surveys, each author is helped to speak more directly to the conflicts, values and beliefs of today's young people.

The significance of this series is enhanced, as well, by the scholarship and commitment of the authors. The grasp of the field in which each writes lends authority to their work and has established this series as a basic reference eagerly read and appreciated by young people.

Contents

Preface

I thought writing this book was going to be easy; it is not. It is difficult to write for young people in this day of turmoil when, as the Angel Gabriel says in Marc Connelly's *Green Pastures,* "Everything nailed down is comin' loose!" I asked myself whether I could put into words something readers, young or not-so-young, might respond to as real in their own lives.

"Words, words, words," said one of my students in this Age of McLuhan. "I am tired of saturating my mind with print. I want a feeling of something real to know first-hand. Sex, for one thing, is so tangible, so *here,* so *now.* I guess that's one thing we can be sure of." I can only hope that my words in this book will make sense to you. Since what I will say is largely out of my own experience with other people and myself, I have some confidence that what I say might touch you where both you and I live.

Since my experience is not yours, I must remain partially outside of your world and you outside of mine. One thing that separates us is our history. I am, in my late forties, a card-carrying member of the "straight" world and I have worked for 25 years with young people as a counselor, teacher and pastor. I am a husband and the father of three daughters in their twenties. I view today's scene through the eyes of one who still has gut-level memories of the depression of the 1930's and with feelings about spending, saving, working, and politics which have been shaped in part by those memories.

"Postpone your pleasure now and prepare for a secure future," was the constant urging of the adults during my childhood. It was useful advice to me and following it (not without conflict—self-discipline comes hard for me) motivated me to acquire the professional credentials to do what I like best to do. But can we give that advice today, in the light of our excessively fragile future? Can we predict or trust in the future direction of society, even if we can shut our eyes to the possibility of world holocaust through war or ecological disaster? It seems to me that, in spite of young people's eruptions into gaiety in "happenings" and rock festivals, their predominant mood is one of grimness, pessimism, and impatience. My oldest daughter had not been in college for more than a few weeks when an assassin's bullet cut down our vibrant, young president in Dallas. That catastrophic event, repeated many times since then, makes normally meaningful events seem irrelevant and trivial.

As a psychotherapist, I see serious faces these days. I hear bitter indictments of parents and country, of university and church, of our industrialized society—in short, the Establishment. Many of these I share. I am made uneasy by the threats of anarchy, of uncontrolled violence, of personal and social chaos expressed in the immediate gratification which sex and drugs seem to offer. I am deeply aware of and responsive to the need for friendship and love. I am awed by the creativity I see in young people. Their desperate search for meaning and for an authentic faith impresses and humbles me.

I am writing this book for two reasons. I want an opportunity to rethink some of my own ideas on the subject of waiting and planning for the future, and I want to share my internal dialogue with any who want to listen. I do not picture myself standing at a lectern or in a pulpit eight feet above contradiction. I will be satisfied if I can increase your own question-asking, your search for answers.

Secondly, I am curious to know if the Christian heritage can have meaning for us in this time of rapid change and challenge to our often unexamined assumptions about life. I will not tack on some "God-talk" as a religious commercial; we have too much "word magic" in our world now. This is the time for honest searching for fidelity, for "something and someone to be true to," as Erik Erikson has said, for something that can give our lives sustaining power, and freedom, and meaning.

I have noticed that, however great the disaffection of young people with the church and the theologies of today, most still are fascinated by Jesus himself. So am I. Repeatedly, for me, he breaks open life again and again to lay bare for me its deepest issues and directions. Where I feel his words may add meaning to this book, I will not hesitate to use them. If we listen to him at all, we must be prepared for surprises. He is not at all the stained-glass figure that much of the church, in its fear, has made him out to be. He had a radical impact on the people of his time, indeed, a revolutionary impact. In contrast, we have used him to support values to which we already are committed. We have dulled the impact of his life by a partial acceptance of his words and his life. If we see him anew, in the midst of our present turmoil, he might very well turn our world upside down (Acts 17:6) and help us reassess our values.

We all play the "waiting game," to some extent, since many aspects of life cannot be forced. *When, how,* and *why* we wait is a crucial matter. A way out of our problem may come in answer to Aldous Huxley's deceptively simple question: "What are people for?"

1.

On Stage—The Now People

This year the students of an affluent suburban high school in California decided to forego a cherished tradition of their yearbook—listing their future plans. A faculty advisor said, "I can't blame them. They're tired of pretending that the boys are going to college, that they're going to become doctors and lawyers, when they face being drafted and perhaps killed."

Whether you feel this way or not, you may agree that when anyone sees only a bleak future ahead, he is tempted to become preoccupied with satisfactions in life *now*. One socially-conscious college student, son of a renowned physicist, put it this way: "Eat, drink and be merry because my father has invented a device that will end the whole business."

Dr. Seymour Halleck, a psychiatrist who works closely with college students, sees enthusiasm for the present as indicating a loss of hope. When students feel powerless to anticipate or direct the future, he says, they adapt by being "cool," and they learn to live in the present without commitments. A degree of demoralization and anxiety has swept over today's college generation and there is reason to believe it is affecting high school students as well.

Why live for the future? Will there even be a future? Many young people are questioning whether there will be an American future, at least. A recent poll, commissioned by "CBS Reports," on the attitudes of college-age young people reported that eight out of 10 saw serious flaws in American society and in the values on which it is based. The Indochina war, racism, and the rape of the natural environment are seen as symptoms of serious illness. A small minority are saying openly that our society's institutions are not capable of change, that they must be destroyed. On the other extreme, a few have succumbed to what Paul Goodman has called the "nothing can be done disease." Even in the university, traditionally a place of freedom of thought and experimentation with new forms, one finds despair growing and curiosity declining.

I am convinced that the *extent* of this unrest among young people is unique, without any parallel in the past, for two reasons: This is the first generation that has never known a time when nuclear war did not threaten total annihilation. Secondly, the turmoil is *world-wide*, as young people are joined together by air travel and TV satellites as they never were before this sophisticated technological age. Young people, with their superior education, understand that continued pollution of water and soil and air can make this planet uninhabitable. Their elders often find this hard to grasp, remembering, as they do, the world of their own childhood and youth.

THE VALUE GAP

The breach between many young people and their elders seems to exist in the degree of urgency that is felt about the reality of this present world crisis. Too many adults see the issue superficially, as obvious differences in life style between the two generations—differences in clothes, hair, rhetoric, and mores. But the changes are much deeper than that. We are seeing the birth of *a new way of life*. The set of values under attack (or at least under critical appraisal) by the "Now Generation" are what Max Lerner calls the five-goal system of American society: success, prestige, money, power, and security. In other words, the heart of the consumer-oriented, business-industrial system in which all of us have grown up. Only one out of five young people polled for "CBS Reports" embraced those values without qualification or apology. This shift is a revolution in goals for living. It is not just a "generation gap" or a "communication gap" or a "stage that the kids are going through." It is a major spiritual crisis. When a large number of the under 25 group—which makes up more than one-half of the population—questions the values on which most of their parents have built their lives (in spite of lip-service to a "Christian way of life") we face, as the National Committee for an Effective Congress put it tersely, "a depression of the national spirit."

One of the chief targets of this challenge of youth is the assumption that the good life requires waiting, self-denial, sacrifice of immediate satisfactions, and long-range planning for the future. Their future seems nebulous and unreal. Self-control and willingness to sacrifice for the future (confident of reward) built both the capitalistic and communistic technological societies. These are the traits necessary for the long, arduous education necessary for any skilled profession. This is the popular version of the Christian way of life a generation ago—a life of self-denial, of self-control (especially of sexual and angry impulses) so that we would please God and ultimately get our reward.

Before World War II, the traditional American and Christian view of life, with its promise of distant rather than immediate pleasures, seemed to be worth any temporary frustration. Sacrifice for future, long-range goals seemed to pay off. But things have changed. To the chagrin of the old-time teacher and preacher, both report card grades and hell (once staples in the motivational arsenal) have lost their effect on many young people. As one teacher complained, "The traditional carrots we hold out to students for delaying their immediate pleasures are seen as rabbit food!"

Today we see a movement away from the future toward the present. A significant number of people are asking, "Why wait, why postpone life? It is here to live now!" This is a message heard from disillusioned college men and women, from tired adults, from professional psychotherapists, and from noted thinkers and writers. This group seems to be gaining in influence. A life of order, of planning, of self-discipline, of achievement is being traded in for what seems to be a life of spontaneity, enjoyment of the present, full expression of feelings, and pleasure and play as worthy goals for living. A different way of looking at life, law, and love is being born, and it offers a powerful vision of a new kind of existence. Yet it is nothing less than heresy to many of the older generation. Mike Nichols' film, "The Graduate," portrays this new man who has run education's obstacle course but is completely turned off by the kind of work in "plastics" that is urged upon him. His real life lies in emotional immediacy and spontaneity of action; no planning ahead means there will be no disappointment. The last scene showing the young couple riding off seems to say, "We do not know where we are going, but we are on the way."

What are some of the pieces in this emerging kaleidoscope of values? What is the distinctive mood which increasing numbers of people share?

THE FLUID LIFE

The currently popular phrase, "hanging loose," says it. Openness is cherished, and there is no desire to shut doors to any experience because of principle. The present is the only reality; the future is unreal and vague. Young people embracing this point of view are hostile to any dogma or any social role which would define their actions or beliefs in advance. In a basic sense they are uncommitted because commitment means making promises for the future. Since one's experience might change, why make up one's mind in advance? You may not feel the same tomorrow. "Happenings" can't be programmed. Young people with this outlook do not work out the clear-cut, long-range plans, or lay out life patterns in advance, as do vocationally-minded students.

Two generations ago it was accepted that a normal life represented a *sequence* of activities, one following another in a somewhat rational order. For example, first you completed your schooling, then you found a job, and then, and only then did you marry. Now it seems desirable to experience all of this at once, and today's affluence makes it possible for some.

The current demand for "relevance" in school is another expression of "nowness." A student may wish to learn only what seems to be related to his current interests, what "grabs him" now. History, to him, is not only boring; it may tie him to old forms of life. Many would like to forget history and begin all over again on a new basis. Nothing, they feel, can be learned from the past. The title of a recent book by young authors says it: "Our Time Is Now."

"Do Your Own Thing"

The cry of the old order was, "Do your duty." Now individuality is stressed, and if there is any sense of duty, it is to one's self, to "self-actualization," to one's real feelings. Appearance, clothing, decorations are the most obvious hallmarks of the new breed: hair, beads, beards, and boots are worn to accentuate individuality, even though they actually have all the elements of a uniform. At a deeper level, individual creations in art, music, poetry, and crafts reveal a distaste for a carbon-copy, mass-produced society.

What is expected, according to social rules, is shunned. A sense of "should" is regarded as a "hang-up." Society's well-established roles are ignored as prisons to the free spirit. There is little desire to live a predictable life, where people can put one in a box, where reactions are automatic. What an older generation would have called perseverance, stick-to-itiveness, and character, in living with an unpleasant situation and seeing it through, the Now People tend to see as a waste of energy. Consequently, they are highly mobile. The notion that life can be better elsewhere—in another city, another family, another relationship, another country, another job, another planet, even another plane of existence—is prevalent. They often discover, however, that while it is easy to change scenes, to flee responsibilities and relationships when they seem burdensome, it is hard to escape them simply by a change of geography. One is left with the same old self on his hands.

Perhaps it was inevitable that "doing your own thing" should have become a popular theme in our highly mechanized culture. When we consider how much of the average American's day is spent in production and consumption, the mechanized "togetherness" in front of the TV which sometimes is called family life, and the increasing sale of sleeping pills, tranquilizers, and other drugs to help us live with tension or to forget that we have not been living, we may find this emphasis on creative individuality good.

The emphasis is on *doing*, and now. While for many young people, the mood is escape, others find in action their reason for being. They want to make a difference. Many see a critical need for immediate action on problems that affect the existence of life itself, but they are tired of canned action, of pre-packaged procedures which seem to stifle the very quality of life which is sought. Most want very much to reestablish the individual over the cost-accounting style of today's bureaucratic society. This is one reason for the ambivalent attitude of young people toward the standard methods of political involvement which are urged upon them. "Do your own thing" may be one way of saying that man should not become a machine.

FOCUS ON FEELINGS

The Today Culture has an appreciation of feelings and sensations totally unknown in the "no-touch" culture in which most of us grew up. In this new psychology, the body and the feelings generated within it are viewed as the most essential aspect of human life. How different from the older generation which viewed the mind as a means of keeping the dangerous body and its impulses under control! The focus upon feelings in an open, honest encounter with another person is the new ideal. The current tide of encounter and sensitivity groups for both young people and adults testifies to the desire to get beyond the overorganized, "up tight" life into a life of feeling. It is also an expression, in my opinion, of the deep loneliness of our time and the need for an intimacy which goes beyond the sharing of ideas and organizational life into a sharing of self and one's emotional secrets.

There are many hazards in this romantic idea that a return to real feelings is the answer to the problems of relationships and of the world. For one thing, the depth of such negative feelings as anger and envy is almost always underestimated. The attempt to escape from hypocrisy and phoniness can lead to self-deception in a new form: pretending that negative feelings do not exist in oneself. Even among the most "beautiful" people, competitiveness and aggression inevitably appear. The reason for laws and social contracts becomes apparent (even in hippie communes): to prevent people from exploiting each other when they are driven by these feelings.

RECOVERING PERSONAL INTIMACY

In the early student protests against universities, the issue was the impersonal quality of the bureaucracy. "Do not bend, spindle, or mutilate" was a phrase found on many a picket sign. Any writer who decries depersonalization in the modern world is given a ready hearing on any campus. The Now People want to create intimate, trusting, open relationships (what one skeptical observer has called "instant I-Thou"). Anything that smacks of rank, social roles, and using people as interchangeable parts in an organization is downright sinful, according to the new code. When a pastor hides behind his collar and a teacher behind his erudition, Now People are "turned off" (it is interesting that this phrase refers to machines).

"Name, rank, and serial number" is what you give your enemies, this generation says; what we want is *you.* Sharing oneself in some circles has become a new *law,* and in many groups great pressure is put upon the person who is reluctant to reveal his inner self. One must feel safe in order to do so, and this often is overlooked.

Power, authority, manipulation, control, or anything else that suggests a one-way relationship is viewed with scorn. The Now People insist on being equal to anyone else, regardless of their training and experience. They often demand direct participation in decision-making. Strongly antiauthoritarian, they despise what they regard as arbitrary, external rules. Since the military is the epitome of this, it is hated above all institutions by many young people.

The recovery of the personal and the hope of ending loneliness is a deep need in our time, but it is hard to come by. There are many substitutes for genuine intimacy. For example, drugs (including alcohol) can be a chemical means to pseudo-intimacy. With them it requires no courage to reach out, beyond one's isolation, to another person, no struggle to reveal, to understand, or to give oneself, as is required in true intimacy. Life's anxieties are diluted, fears are dulled, defenses and inhibitions are anesthetized, and one seems to be a part of the world painlessly, without effort. All of this may lead to a spurious, rather than a real, intimacy.

"Chaste makes waste" reads a button worn by a member of the Now Generation. Sex is perhaps most often explored as the path to personal intimacy in our day. The pattern is not always one of promiscuity but may consist of "meaningful" relationships, with the young people who are involved often feeling that "sex is right and natural for people who are good to each other." The tremendous increase in "mini-marriages," men and women living together without legal ties, testifies to the search for genuine intimacy.

REJECTION OF WORK

The Protestant work ethic is under attack from many sides. Challenged is the assumption that our main identity as human beings is determined by how well we perform at our jobs. Many young people no longer are lured to a job by either the money or the status it offers. This is hard to understand for a generation which sought life's meaning in work. But a new day and a

new mood are upon us. The Academy of Science is predicting
that by the 1980's a four-hour work day will be the pattern for
many types of work. With our work week already cut by 50
per cent since the turn of the century, this change is not hard
to imagine. What will happen if we no longer can depend upon
the old values of hard work, self-denial, and living toward some
future fulfillment of one's work? What if play, meditation,
leisure, and personal relationships begin to take the place of
work as a way of life? The Now People, emphasizing the enjoyment of life as an alternative to meaningless labor, quote with
approval Ecclesiastes 1:3: "What does man gain by all the toil
at which he toils under the sun?"

We do not know how our society, with its "gospel of success," will be transformed if its fundamental assumptions about
work no longer exist. For example, "a man should get out of
life only what he puts into it by work." Or, "only those who
have earned their way by hard work are worthy of respect; the
rest are parasites and drifters." When a man is measured not
by his achievements but by his personal qualities, when he no
longer cares to "win," what will happen to us as a people? This
dilemma is captured in a cartoon in which a career counselor is
saying to a long-haired hippie: "And have you had any experience besides 'grooving'?"

BEYOND TRIBAL LOYALTIES

The Now Generation is not inclined to draw lines between
groups of people as were their parents who had a pretty clear
idea of who they thought was acceptable and who was not. In
fact, the Now Generation is deeply incensed by artificial barriers between people created by nationality, law, education,
race, and the like. Many youth today want contact with every
kind of person, no matter how alien they may be to their parents' way of life: the deprived, the poor, the politically alien,
the non-white, the deformed, etc. In fact, those who are different often are more attractive than those who are familiar. Because they grew up with Christianity, they will give it no hear-

ing, but strange new faiths are given full attention. The nationality of people or ideas matter little: Zen Buddhism, French existentialism, Indian mysticism, Yugoslavian communism all are candidates for a new blend of meaning in their lives. Avid travelers, they become intense internationalists and are particularly critical of the kind of patriotism that claims superiority of one nation over others.

Here, then, are some of the ingredients of a new way of life. Some would see in these emerging values the wave of the future, the making of a new type of human being. At the very least, some of the cherished assumptions of our culture are being challenged by an intelligent, active minority of young people. In some ways, these are not new values at all. The historian or the philosopher may see the Now Man as representing a conflict between the ancient Greek ways of Dionysus (the strange, wild, dancing God) and Apollo (the god of reasonableness, order, discipline and balance). The popularity of Kazantzakis' *Zorba the Greek* is testimony to the growing ascendency of the Dionysian way. Zorba dances when the joy or tragedy of life outraces his capacity for words.

The emergence of the Now People with their new consciousness of life must be taken seriously, even though we may challenge many of the ways they seek new life. We can appreciate the *desire* for the freedom which characterizes the new style without buying the *prescriptions* for freedom which are advanced by some of the young people. For example, the hippie seeks to destroy the inhibitions that he thinks have kept him fettered, while the anarchist of the New Left seeks to destroy the social rules, institutions, and practices that he feels have inhibited his self-expression and development. Each places strong emphasis upon freedom *from* restraint, but relatively little emphasis on what freedom is *for*.

A Christian has a vantage point from which to look at any movement because he believes he has a picture of authentic human life in Jesus of Nazareth. In the light of the changing values just described, ponder these words of the late Samuel

Miller, dean of Harvard Divinity School, as he contrasts Jesus'
life style and our own:

"He was careless about himself, we are careful. He was cou-
rageous, we are cautious. He trusted the untrustworthy, we
trust those who have good collateral. He forgave the unfor-
giveable, we forgive those who do not really hurt us. He was
righteous and laughed at respectability, we're respectable
and laugh at righteousness. He was meek, we are ambitious.
He saved others, we save ourselves as much as we can. He
had no place to lay his head, and did not worry about it,
while we fret because we do not have the last convenience
manufactured by clever science. He did what he believed to
be right regardless of consequences, while we determine
what is right by how it will affect us. He feared God but not
the world. We fear public opinion more than we fear the
judgment of God. He risked everything for God, we make
religion a refuge from every risk . . . He was a scandal, a
scandal to the Jews, proud of their tradition, a scandal to the
scribes, proud of the Law, a scandal to the priests, proud of
the Temple, a scandal to his family, proud of their respectability, a scandal to the disciples, proud of their ambi-
tions." *

It is just possible that he is the Man for us.

* Samuel H. Miller, *The Life of the Church.* New York: Harper and
Bros., 1953, pp. 46 ff.

2.

The Time of Your Life— Now or Then?

In what tense do you live? Do you spend most of your time in awareness of what is going on around and within you now? Or is much of your energy used in remembering the past, or anticipating your future? When I am enjoying life or the actual activity in which I am engaged, I give little thought to past or future. It is *now* that counts. But when I am frustrated or lonely, or engaged in work that is drudgery, my mind either wanders off into the past or leaps into the months or years ahead. When things are not going well, I find myself (like Lot's wife) looking back to happier days. Sometimes when we are thrust into a new situation—college, a new job, a new place to live, new people to meet—we may recall how good life used to be. We may either idealize the past, or remember past failures and anxieties. We may rehearse former triumphs, caress favorite memories to neutralize our fear of the new. We also may escape imaginatively into the future. "Someday, when I am married and settled down. . . ." "When I finish my degree. . . ." "When the war is over . . . I'll start to live." And we try to daydream our way out of frustrations of the moment instead of meeting them head on.

It is inevitable that we commute between the three time zones—past, present, future—of our lives. The real question is, which is home base? I think the *present* is home base, but past and future also are needed to give full meaning to our existence. Understanding the true purpose of each dimension, we can avoid wasting a great deal of energy in living.

Preoccupation with future or past is self-defeating. Magic hopes, fantastic plans, empty dreams, and ungrounded fears and worries can rob us of the freedom to live creatively and fully now. Overconcern with the past is equally paralyzing.

Jesus was speaking to those who were trying to anticipate and to guarantee their futures when he said:

> "Don't worry and don't keep saying, 'What shall we eat, and what shall we drink or what shall we wear?' That is what pagans are always looking for; your Heavenly Father knows that you need them all. Set your heart on his kingdom and his goodness and all these things will come to you as a matter of course. Don't worry at all then about tomorrow. Tomorrow can take care of itself. One day's trouble is enough for one day." (Matthew 6:31–34, New English Bible).

At the same time Jesus recognized that we must plan realistically for the future. He expressed this in his parable about the building of the tower, found in Luke 14. His viewpoint was basically this: "Be thankful for what *has* happened to bring you to this point in life, instead of being overanxious about what *might* happen in the future. That future is in God's hands."

Escape from the Present

A neurotic person's life is not lived fully in the present. For him the present is not happy, and he feels that if anything is possible at all, it must lie in the future. He is impatient with the present; he kills time, fleeing mentally to the hoped-for satisfactions of tomorrow. He cannot give himself to what he is doing now.

Bob, a college student, is an example. He feels apathetic, empty, without well-defined goals. He says, "I can't make myself want to study." When he sits at his desk, he becomes anxious, fearful that he cannot achieve well enough to win his father's and his own approval. The more anxious he becomes, the more he indulges in vague daydreaming, like Walter Mitty. Or he will join any friend who happens to come by and suggests doing anything but studying. He imagines although vaguely what he might be some day, but does not take the first practical step toward realizing his dreams. His disappointments in not doing his best lead to increased daydreaming and escape, which in turn decrease his efficiency. He runs away from the present into a world of fantasy.

In contrast to Bob, Jane lives in the past by blaming others for her problems. Like many past-oriented persons, she labors under feelings of guilt, self-hatred, and resentment. She keeps remembering and rehearsing past hurts. She imagines what might have been. She says, "This is what they have made me; how do you expect me to change?" Jane plays the "if only" game: "if only I had had different parents;" "if only I had been born with a different body;" "if only. . . ." She devotes herself to the pursuit of safety. When she makes decisions, she wants above all to protect herself against anything that might be dangerous. She knows what she wants to *avoid*, but she is vague about what she wants to achieve, and how to develop her real potential.

From these brief descriptions, we can see that much of our tendency to live in the past or to jump ahead into the future is born of fear. Do not misunderstand. There is nothing wrong in occasionally remembering the past or in anticipating, imagining, and planning for the future. When we deliberately choose to remember or to plan, that is very different from wandering off into the past or the future as a *substitute* for living with the present. Now check yourself. While reading these paragraphs, how many times did your mind leave what you were reading to drift into past memories or future fantasies? Try to remember what your thoughts were. Write them down. They represent "unfinished business" that you will have to complete for yourself, deep yearnings that still are alive in you.

How can you know when you are living in the present?

When you are able to *concentrate* on what you are doing and to *listen.* When you are writing a paper, reading a book, listening to music, or engaging in conversation, and, whatever your activity, you are fully devoted to it at that moment and it is the only thing that matters. When you cannot think of the next thing to be done because you are doing something right now. When it doesn't matter so much *what* you are doing, as long as you give yourself to it fully.

It is so easy to place our bodies in one location and our minds a hundred miles away, preoccupied with something else. It is difficult to concentrate when almost everything distracts us—noise, music, travel. It is strange and uncomfortable to be alone without doing something just to "keep busy."

Listening to others and to ourselves is another test of living in the present. How seldom we hear each other deeply! It is a rare experience when people truly hear us—our surface talk, as well as our feelings underneath—when someone cares enough to listen closely. This means that someone is there, where we live, and this makes a relationship come alive. Read Matthew 26:36–46, the story of Jesus' suffering in Gethsemane. His disciples failed him three times during that agonizing time by drowsing off, by not being fully present. In this deepest terror of his life, they could not be *with* him. Tragically, many of us are in a "Gethsemane sleep," a drowse of preoccupation or distraction, much of the time, and we completely miss the suffering of people around us.

It is surprising how many people cannot listen to *themselves;* they do not know what they feel. They are alienated from their center. They may know what they *should* feel, or what they *think* they feel, but not what they *actually* feel, whether it is anxiety, gratitude, anger, joy, excitement, or whatever. They become detached from themselves. As Kierkegaard said, "The 'I' is deadened to such a point that it lives in the third person." Even their language shows how detached they are from their feelings and their body. For example, here is the way a counselor might work with a boy to help him "own" his own body and experience. Note the way he avoids using the word "I" by recourse to "it" and other impersonal words:

"What are you experiencing now?"

"My foot is making this movement . . ."

"Is *it* making the movement?"

"I am moving my foot like this . . . and the feeling comes to me . . ."

"The feeling *comes to* you?"

"*I feel* . . . well, I know I use 'it' and impersonal ways of speaking about myself and I'm glad you're bringing it to my attention. I'm grateful for this."

"*This?*"

"Your idea."

"My idea?"

"*I feel grateful to you.*"

Do you notice the circuitous route the boy takes in expressing his own feelings? This process of owning one's body and expressing one's feelings directly is very difficult for those who do not live in the present, and who do not feel comfortable with themselves. They treat themselves as objects. They are detached.

Zest in living comes from concentrating on the present, from living and viewing every second afresh, unlike any moment which has gone before. This contrasts vividly with the past-oriented person to whom one of T. S. Eliot's characters said in *The Cocktail Party*, "You are nothing but a set of obsolete responses."

IMPRISONED IN THE PRESENT

We have spoken of living in the "now," with a sense of immediacy about life. Clearly, here is where most of our energies ought to be. But total involvement in the present, without guidelines from past and future, can also be destructive. To grasp the present moment only, forgetting the past and despairing of the future, robs life of its meaning. Real life cannot stay alive in a mere succession of "nows," in a one-dimensional world. To be human, man must reach out from the present to snatch handfuls of the past and of the future; he must learn to "bind" time together. There is a vast difference between living *for* the present and living *in* the present.

Would any of us doubt that our anticipation of the future has a bearing on how we live now? Listen to this description of the viewpoint of a pessimistic existentialist and ask yourself how you would live in the present if you were he:

> "The world is evil. It's in the power of overpowering brutality and force. So I cannot shape the world as I would like to have it. I have now come to see that the future cannot be shaped by my hand and therefore in a sense the future is not important anymore. In fact, there *is* no such thing as the future. The only thing that man can know is the present moment. The future? What is it? It is but the false and delusionary projections people carry around in their minds. It has no reality; it is only an idea. The only reality is the present moment of my experience. Therefore I am going to fill the present moment to its full . . . The right now is the only existence anybody has. For life is not a future; life is but a movement towards death. . . ." *

Countless people feel that way today, expecting either a catastrophe or a bleak future. How much of this statement is realism and how much is sheer pessimism is hard to say. But unless a person *believes* he won't be dead before morning, his present becomes sour.

Personal goals for the future seem to be necessary to healthful living. Without them one is the victim of random, meaningless action and the search for kicks. The person imprisoned in the present engages in a compulsive drive to experience ev-

* From an unpublished paper by Dr. Ross Snyder of Chicago Theological Seminary: "Shapes of Mind in People Today."

erything, and as quickly as possible. He is impatient. The need for instant results and instant intimacy prevails. And with the satiation of appetites, a heavy dose of boredom can set in. As the author of Proverbs wrote, "Where there is no vision, the people perish." Clear goals are part of the nourishment human beings demand. One of our best-known psychologists, the late Gordon Allport, put it this way:

> "The possession of long-range goals, regarded as central to one's personal existence, distinguishes the human being from the animal, the adult from the child, and in many cases, the healthy person from the sick." *

It's easy enough to talk about living fully in the present, but what if the present is so restricted and frustrating that any action is virtually impossible? Then one's vision of the future can keep one alive and creative. When St. Paul wrote the letter to the Romans, the score was Lions 6, Christians 0. Terror, torture, and death dogged the footsteps of that minority group called "Christians" in the first and second centuries, A.D. They possessed almost nothing but faith, hope and love as their defense. It was in these times that Paul wrote:

> ". . . Whatever we have to go through now is less than nothing compared with the magnificent future God has planned for us. The hope is that in the end the whole of created life will be rescued from the tyranny of change and decay, and have its share in that magnificent liberty which can only belong to the children of God . . . It is plain to anyone with eyes to see that at the present time all of life groans in a sort of universal travail. And it is plain, too, that we who have a foretaste of the Spirit are in a state of painful tension, while we wait for that redemption . . . In our moments of impatience let us remember that hope always means waiting for what we haven't yet got . . . The Spirit

* Gordon Allport, *Becoming*. New Haven: Yale University Press, 1955, p. 51.

of God not only maintains this hope in us but helps us in our present limitations. For example, we do not know how to pray . . . but his Spirit within us is actually praying for us in those agonizing longings which never find words . . ." (Romans 8:18 ff. Phillips Translation).

This Christian understanding of hope stands in stark contrast to the pessimistic picture of the existentialist given earlier.

The autobiographical accounts of concentration camp experiences written by Victor Frankl in *From Death Camp to Existentialism*, Bruno Bettelheim in *The Informed Heart*, and Ernest Gordon in *Through the Valley of the Kwai* show that hope for the future stimulates endurance and creative activity in seemingly hopeless situations. A study completed in the 1950's of 6,000 Americans imprisoned during the Korean War showed that 30 per cent of them died in captivity, compared with 1 per cent who died in prison in Europe during World War II.

Medical observers reported that the cause of death during the Korean War was, in many instances, ill-defined and could best be described as "give-up-itis." Being imprisoned caused serious demoralization, humiliation, and deprivation of human support. Many prisoners became apathetic, listless, neither ate nor drank, stared into space, and finally died. Apparently they felt they had no future to look forward to, nor did they believe anyone cared. Those who did come out alive (and later became effective persons) tended to view their imprisonment as a painful interruption of life. They were convinced they would come out alive, that someone cared, and they focused on life as it was to be lived in the future. Plans were made for future jobs, for marriage and a family. These plans often were developed in great detail, including house blueprints, education, even future entertainment, including barbecue menus. The present was not the only reality for these prisoners of war. The philosopher, Abraham Kaplan, has said, "I am defined not by what I have but by what I seek; the aspiration is the man!" These experiences illustrate Nietzsche's point that "he who has a *why* to live for can bear almost any *how*."

The future and its pull cannot so easily be squeezed out of the life of a healthy person. Nor can we ignore a sense of the past without dire consequences. It is not ordinarily recognized how our memories of our own pasts help us know who we are. A psychologist performed a vivid experiment that supports this view. He hypnotized a young man and suggested that he would have no awareness of his future when he was returned to consciousness. When he came out of the hypnotic trance, he was carefree, even giddy. No anxieties plagued him. (This bears out one psychologist's idea that anxiety is the gap between the "now" and later). Then the young man was hypnotized again, and it was suggested that, upon awakening, his past would have been erased. The result was startling. He sat in a catatonic stupor; a blank stare greeted the experimenter. He could not talk or show feeling. Having lost his past, he also had lost his sense of identity and aliveness.

I wonder if the loss of a sense of history is part of our problem today. Margaret Mead believes that what young people want is to begin over again, to leave the past behind, to repudiate what their elders are doing now. One cannot get rid of the past quite that easily. Look first at one's personal life. My own personality today contains much I have learned from my past; it is impossible to simply shake this off. My habits, ways of looking at things, reactions to persons and situations, my speech, my thoughts, my loves, my hates all have been inscribed (deeply, if not indelibly) upon my psyche by past experiences. These experiences also have greatly influenced my attitude toward the future, my anticipations, hopes, and fears. Anyone who thinks he can escape the "styling" that past influences have contributed to him is fooling himself. When a person says, "I am I," he is acknowledging the uniqueness that has been shaped by his own personal history. To be sure, you are not condemned to repeat automatically the patterns established in the past. As you become aware of the purpose these patterns serve, you also can become, to a certain extent, free of their power. But more than you may realize, your past is with you now.

People need historical roots. The search for the history of one's name is fascinating because it helps to establish a link with the past. We want to identify with something more permanent than the latest model car. Perhaps today's revival of interest in astrology, and its effort to discover direction through the movement of the stars, is an attempt to escape the sense of cosmic lostness, to establish a link with something more permanent than a whim.

I am saying that we all need both a sense of history, of our past, as well as of our future to give meaning to the present moment. To live in a barren succession of "nows," without a sense of where we have been and where we are going, is too confining for the human spirit. Man is a time-binding being; he must put his past, his present, and his future together in some meaningful way. As the theologians say, he is incurably "eschatological." That is, he needs a vision of where all life is heading, where it will come out, and how he fits into the picture, even if he cannot know the details.

What happens when a person tries to live totally in the present? Since he denies himself the zest of action directed toward a goal, he must look for artificial spurs to his awareness, his excitement. Imprisoned in the present, he desperately seeks experiences which he thinks give life drama and bite. LSD and other hallucinogens sometimes give him the experiences of a new perceptual world and a sense of timelessness. Tragically, chronic drug users (in contrast to those who temporarily use drugs under the care of physicians) often exhibit growing passivity; they no longer decide what they are becoming but drift and wait for experiences to carry them along, to give them a sense of significance. The psychedelic world may take the place of active, creative work toward the future. If the world ceases to be stimulating, the chronic user is lost and bored. He easily progresses into despair and depression. Living in one time zone —the present—is not enough.

A QUESTION OF TIMING

Not everything can be experienced now. The time is not ripe for all things to be experienced at all times. Some things can't be forced. You can't force a tree to grow. This is one of the biblical insights that the modern world seems to have forgotten. Measuring time solely by past, present, and future is "clock time," or *chronos*, in Greek. But the Greeks had another word for time: *kairos*, which is closest in meaning to the English word, "timing." *Kairos* means the unique moment in time in which something could happen or could be accomplished. Ecclesiastes states the point memorably:

"For everything has its season, and for every activity under heaven its time:

a time to be born and a time to die;
a time to plant and a time to uproot;
a time to kill and a time to heal;
a time to pull down and a time to build up;
a time to weep and a time to laugh;
a time for mourning and a time for dancing;
a time to scatter stones and a time to gather them;
a time to embrace and a time to refrain from embracing;
a time to seek and a time to lose;
a time to keep and a time to throw away;
a time to tear and a time to mend;
a time for silence and a time for speech;
a time to love and a time to hate;
a time for war and a time for peace." (Ecclesiastes 3:1–8
New English Bible).

Not every moment of the present is *kairos*. When is the time ripe for a particular activity or event? How can we tell? We can never be as sure as when we pick the fruit that is ripe. But intuitively we feel it is more fulfilling to do things (loving, planting, speaking) at one time rather than another. This is why concentration on the present is not the total answer. The impulse to do something now is only half of the picture. It may or may not be appropriate or even possible to do something at the time one wishes. Sometimes a conscious wish must be sacrificed to reality and appropriate timing. If we understand this, the words "delay," "wait," "hope," "plan" may not seem to have been designed by malevolent, old law-givers to frustrate the young. They may actually be the means to fulfillment and joy, if properly interpreted. Wait until the time is ripe.

THE THREE-DIMENSIONAL MAN

Now, before we go further, please read the 13th chapter of Paul's first letter to the Corinthians, preferably in a modern translation such as Phillips or the New English Bible: "In a word, there are three things that last forever: faith, hope, and love; but the greatest of them all is love."

Familiar as this passage is, few people recognize that St. Paul actually is speaking of man in three dimensions of time when he speaks of "faith, hope, and love." These are not competing qualities of character but ways in which Christians bind past, future, and present together in a meaningful way.

Faith gives meaning to the present by drawing its reality from past events, specifically the biblical accounts of the Exodus of the Jews out of Egypt and the life, death, and resurrection of Jesus Christ. The Exodus and Easter are crucial in understanding life because they both point to *liberation*, to freedom from a bondage that would keep us from being fully human. Christ gave us new hope, not for escape from this world into another, but for a share in the victory over the power of evil in the world and in our own lives. This participation is real, although incomplete in the here-and-now. That is why Christians pray, "Thy Kingdom come, thy will be done on earth, as it is in heaven." In worship we celebrate those crucial liberating events of the past; we make them a reality of the present. The freedom the believer sees in Jesus becomes the truest thing about life, a truth that finally will prevail among all men.

What is *love?* Love (*agape'*) is a demonstration of faith *in the present*, faith that one is liberated, freed. In love we demonstrate freedom from the defensive, self-protective attitudes that keep us from entering into the lives of others, to listen with compassion, to care. Walled-in defensiveness leads to the self-imposed loneliness of a loveless life. It is deadening. But as the author of I John wrote, "We know that we have passed from death to life because we love . . ." Love, because it means personal caring *now*, is "the greatest of them all."

The Christian's *hope* is not wild speculation based on longing. What we hope for has some reality here and now. There is a continuity of past, present, and future in our hope. The last chapter of this book will deal more fully with hope.

Christians know they cannot rush life; they must wait for the right time to act. Yet they do act, they do take part in a life that has its past, its history—with banners and beaconfires, heroes and martyrs—its present, and its future. None of the three time zones can be squeezed out of that drama, but it is clear which is the most important.

LINKING PRESENT TO FUTURE

There are several ways you can deal with your future. You can dream, you can anticipate events with a sense of impending doom, or you can be unrealistically optimistic that everything will turn out beautifully. And you can plan. Planning is the function of the mind that I want to talk about, because this is the most helpful way of dealing with the future. Not that daydreaming is all bad. Sometimes it is fun to lose yourself in the fantasies, however unrealistic, that parade through your mind. You can learn about your personal needs from your day-dreams.

Do you dream of being famous? Realizing, then, that your need for recognition is strong, you'll plan for a way to satisfy it. But you also must learn to organize your energies, and to face the unpleasant situations you try to overcome by daydreaming.

Planning is something quite different. It is the "first step on a journey of a thousand miles." Planning means distinguishing between present and future, between the way things are and the way they might be. This distinction is not popular among the Now Generation. Planning cannot be rigid; it is not a straight jacket, as in totalitarian nations with their penchant for five and 10-year plans. Planning in this sense is of no use because life is dynamic and cannot be forced into any mold we choose. (What organism *plans* its growth, its life? And yet the human being has more options than plants or lower animals to choose among).

Plans should be guidelines, direction-finders only, and changed if they thwart rather than promote life. Our problem is that, without a life plan, we half-heartedly move along, we drift. As pressures mount, we change direction again and again. We will deal with goal-setting in detail in the next chapter, but as we close this one we should keep in mind that planning makes it possible and necessary to link present and future.

Because so many of the Now Generation see life-planning as diametrically opposed to the spontaneity in the here-and-now which they seek, I want to express my own convictions about planning for the future. I see life-planning as:

> crucial
> deliberate
> realistic
> flexible.

CRUCIAL

Unless you try to employ purpose and planning to bind the present to the future, your options for life later on will be much narrower than they might have been. How you decide to use your time now affects not only the quality of your life now, but also the freedom you will have in the future. Modern psychological literature abounds in phrases like "self-actualization," "realizing one's full potential." Such jargon doesn't help us face the fact that no one can realize *all* of his potentialities. If he chooses to develop some of his talents, he may have to deny others. Time and energy are limited; we are finite creatures. When we say "yes" to one avenue of endeavor, we must say "no" to its alternatives. So our early choices (for example, whether to stay in school, or to leave home, or to get married now, etc.) may severely limit our freedom later on.

I know this is difficult for many of the Now Generation to understand. There is little inclination to make choices that favor the long as against the short run. This generation is asking if there will be a "long run." And although that long run may seem remote and unreal, human beings have been given the gift of imagination and forethought to do what lower animals cannot do. I can decide to plan for what exists now only in my imagination. I can *create a reality which will not exist unless I bring it about by my own activity*. It is my conviction that young people need long-range aspirations that are tied realistically to their present activity. They must act *as if* a future is possible. Middle-aged men and women (who, in increasing numbers are seeing psychotherapists, often because their lives seem meaningless) must give more attention to present experiences instead of to future goals, but for young people, life-planning is crucial. It means that you are taking the responsibility for designing and working toward a satisfying future life.

DELIBERATE

It is wise, occasionally, to reflect on the past and project one's future as a guide to present action. For example: "Thinking back over the last couple of semesters, I have found that I can work 30 hours a week and take six units a semester at such-and-such a college. I can't do more than that without spreading my life too thin. It looks as if I can finish up an Associate of

Arts degree in four years, if I decide to keep up the present pace."

A great deal of time and money is being spent these days by government and business groups to project an image of the future that will guide present efforts. Should an individual, then, simply drift and let events and a school time-table determine his future? Planning for the future determines the development of his personality and his life quite as effectively as do the forces of the past.

A psychologist recently did a research study of effective and non-effective young adults in the Peace Corps. He asked them to write autobiographies of their future lives, in a fictionalized form. He found that the young people who later were highly rated on their overseas performances described their futures differently from those who proved to be ineffective. The effective Peace Corpsman was able to describe his future in considerable detail. He saw himself as working hard to reach his goal and shape his life. Planning had become a deliberate part of his life.

REALISTIC

Planning for one's future certainly does not mean trying to achieve an idealized image of oneself, or playing a certain role in life; it must be realistic—concentrated on the full use of the real self. Living for an idealized image of oneself is one sure way to kill life. That is just what Jesus said: "He who seeks to save his life will lose it; and he who loses his life for my sake will find it."

The important thing is to start with what you are and where you are. You may feel inadequate when you compare yourself with your wished-for self, but that self is pure fantasy. It is better to say with Noah in the play, *Green Pastures*, "I ain't very much, but I'se all I got." There is no end to the self-torture and misery you can inflict upon yourself if you insist on comparing yourself with some ideal. If you are a perfectionist, you are sunk before you take your first step because you always will be disappointed and you always will have the opportunity to criticize yourself. No, the trick, as I see it, is to orchestrate your hangups, your strengths, and your vision into a realistic picture of what you might do and how you can usefully operate. No one has said it better than Emerson:

> "There is a time in every man's education when he arrives at the conviction that envy is ignorance; that imitation is suicide; that he must take himself for better, for worse, as his portion; that though the wide universe is full of good, no kernel of nourishing corn can come to him but through his toil bestowed on that plot of ground which is given to him to till." *

Aspirations that do not fit you and your situation are hopeless projects. Realistic planning builds on your genuine interests and abilities and on what fits you in your deepest nature.

FLEXIBLE

All of life cannot be made to fit into a procrustean bed of our expectations. A blueprint of life cannot be laid out in advance; only the guidelines which make sense to you now can be set. A plan cannot guarantee that such-and-such *will* happen or *must* happen. Such certainty is never possible for us. Life is a risk and an adventure. Furthermore, none of our plans or purposes, however important they might seem at the moment, are irrevocable. Since this is your plan and your time, it can be changed as circumstances lead you to see your decision in a different light. Having decided on a college major, for example, you might find exciting possibilities that suggest another direction. It always is possible for you to reopen the question; that is part of your freedom.

Flexibility demands that we not map out all the details for the rest of our lives, but that we take things one step at a time.

* "Self-Reliance," *Works of Ralph Waldo Emerson*, London, 1905, p. 10.

The famous psychologist, Kurt Lewin, discovered that the effective individual set his next goal somewhat, but not too much, above his last achievement. He stayed close to the reality of his experience. The ineffective person, on the other hand, either set his goal too low because he anticipated failure, or so far above his proven ability that he could achieve only in fantasy and day-dreams. Whether an individual stays with his goal depends on two factors: the value of the goal to him, and his belief that his goal is within his reach, that he actually can achieve it.

There is a way of living fully *in* the present without living *for* the present. Freedom is your power to tie together the present and succeeding moments, months, and years by purposeful planning. To answer the question, "What is the time of your life?", it is both now *and* then.

3.

The New Four Letter
Word:—Work

Is the Today Generation anti-work? Has *Playboy's* playboy replaced Horatio Alger as the hero of youth? Those people who lived through the Great Depression of the 1930's tend to say, "yes." The terror of losing your property and savings, of having no paycheck coming in, of suddenly becoming dependent upon others for survival, of feeling like a failure, leaves an indelible impression on you and your view of life. Most of those who suffered through that experience reacted by thinking that job security and money were the most important things in life. It is hard for them to understand why young people today put so little weight on these two values and upon the self-discipline and the drive for achievement necessary to attain them.*

Today the average college or college-bound young person (the ghettoized black youth being an outstanding exception) has lived all his life in affluence. He seldom has been deprived of anything, except living in terror of poverty. Working-class young people are not as likely to reject affluence and money as values because they haven't "made it" yet. Many college students, on the other hand, seem to be rejecting the very things for which the less fortunate still are striving. That is one reason

* See Studs Terkel's latest book, *Hard-times: An Oral History of the Great Depression*. Pantheon, 1970.

college students are so deeply resented by many rank-and-file citizens today.

But this analysis is not the whole story. It is true that many readers of this book have grown up in families where abundance, economic security, and freedom of expression are facts of life, not goals to strive for. But by living in such affluence, many have come to question the quality of life in an atmosphere of indulgence. Young people who have little or no emotional investment in the material things of life actually may be better able to say what they think about the quality of life their parents' struggle has purchased. And they are raising serious questions about the common goals of profit, power, and prestige.

The Reluctantly Committed

Nevertheless, those who are not radicals calling for revolutionary change in society may be reluctantly committed to their parents' way of life. They may play according to the rules of the acquisitive society—they compete, they push ahead academically and athletically for future rewards, they are not averse to "wheels" or to leisure-filled week-ends as the "good life." Like their parents, they even may want to "get ahead and make a name for themselves." Yet they experience increasing uneasiness about the meaning and satisfaction of such a route. Many young people genuinely are distressed that they might resemble their parents. They often see their parents as driven, as empty, as oriented to things and to conspicuous consumption. That view may be one-sided, but there is a revulsion against a life which seems so devoid of genuine pleasure. They sense the "surburban sadness," the vast sameness, the lack of passion for causes and indignation about injustice and waste and pollution. (They may overlook their parents' passion because it is quieter than their own). And so young people wish there were goals, values, and institutions to which they *could* be genuinely committed.

In their search, many experiment with the "expansion of

consciousness" methods of self-understanding, esthetic experiences, and personal openness. Even as they seek these qualities, they are asking whether it is morally right to do so when much of the world, and many Americans, live in deprivation and depression. However, there may be deep wisdom in this "interior journey" of young people. The English historian, Arnold Toynbee, in A *Study of History* speaks of withdrawal-and-return. He writes that when a civilization comes to "a time of troubles," such as we are now in, a significant number of people turn from the outer world of political and social chaos to the inner world of the psyche, and there they come upon a vision of a new way of life. Then they return to the outer world to form the nucleus of a "creative minority" through which civilization can find renewal.

It is abundantly clear that many young men are no longer interested in proving their manhood on the greens of a golf course or on water-skis. Many go through the motions of the "successful," but without any conviction that the motions have meaning. Clearly, large numbers of young men are challenging the well-established work ethic which says that one's vocation, leading to achievement and prestige, is the purpose of life. Furthermore, they resent pressure from parents to join the rat-race of relentless competition and achievement by choosing a career early (sometimes a career a parent wishes he had followed). Not only is this tactic self-defeating, since each of us must find our own way at our own pace, but it is impossible. The prediction now is being made that a young person may need to be educated to hold successively three, four, or even a half-dozen, different kinds of jobs in the course of his lifetime. Who can foresee what the shape of the professions will be?

Alvin Toffler, in his new book, *Future Shock*, comments that the average mother has no idea what she is talking about when she says she would like to see Johnny become a lawyer. "Jurimetrics," a product of the computer revolution, will have changed the profession beyond recognition in another decade. It involves electronic data processing, information storage, and retrieval which can make immediately available all relevant legal precedents, as well as analyze legal decisions. Will mother recognize the lawyer of the future?

It is my conviction that most of today's young people are not protesting against work, but against *meaningless* work. Further, they accept meaningful work as a *part* of life, but they don't want it to dominate every other activity.

Competence vs. Style

I think there is a strong drive for competence in the human being, for the sense of being able to do something well, of being able to influence his environment in some way. A child must experience a wonderful sense of discovery when he finds out what effect he has on what objects. His growing sense of competence contributes to his self-esteem. Adolescents also respect competence. I suspect that one reason for the phenomenal appeal of the early James Bond movies was the competence Bond exhibited in everything, from thinking, to fighting, to loving. Young people know it is not enough to get along with people, to "groove" with them. Respect for real competence— in the classroom, the shop, the street, the driver's seat, on the rock festival stage—is the foundation of meaningful work. Unless one has been defeated early in life, or because of feelings of guilt sets himself up for one failure after another, a human being's need for competence is strong. Man enjoys being competent.

But a new type of young person is emerging who values syle over competency. Psychiatrists are seeing him in increasing numbers. He complains of boredom, of hang-ups, of just going through the motions. He is intelligent, verbally fluent, and smooth. He talks much about "life style." And he *is* a stylist. By this I mean that he relies upon social techniques and maneuvers to sell himself. He values style over content, over the mastery of any skill or any area of knowledge. He'd rather free-associate into a tape recorder for a teacher than do the exacting work for a term paper or a research project. One quickly learns that he cannot deal in depth with any problem, including his own. He has rejected the planning and sustained effort necessary for competence, or for dealing thoroughly with issues. Because he is imprisoned in the present, and because he hates any denial of immediate pleasure, he moves from one experience to another but he experiences nothing deeply. One week he is "into haiku," the next week "into Marcuse," a third week "into leather-crafting." But his poems and projects are never completed; the books are never read beyond the first chapter. He is a sampler, a stylist who has turned his back on his own need for competency and the sense of meaning it can give.

IS WORK A DIRTY WORD?

Since, then, we enjoy being competent, and need to be competent, why is it that so many of us have a negative feeling toward work? A clue comes to us in the common usage of the word. The 1967 edition of *Webster's Unabridged Dictionary* defines work as "activity in which one exerts strength or faculties to do or perform: a. sustained physical or mental effort valued as it overcomes obstacles and achieves an objective or result . . . ; b. the labor, task, or duty that affords one his accustomed means of livelihood . . . ; c. strenuous activity marked by the presence of difficulty and exertion and absence of pleasure . . ." Notice how effort, obstacles, and lack of pleasure are emphasized.

Missing entirely in this definition is the idea that work can be carried on without undue strain, and that it often can be pleasurable and fulfilling. In *36 Children*, a sensitive and dedicated teacher described his unforgettable year in a ghetto classroom. A group of fearful, unresponsive, moody youngsters expected to do "school work" was transformed into excited, eager, happy learners. As he tapped their deepest interests, their participation and creativity were awakened. Unfortunately, the home, the street, and the society to which these children returned after school killed the spark that was kindled in all but a very few.

A common understanding of the work ethic is that one always must put work ahead of play. Indeed, play or leisure (the two often are erroneously equated) is justified only because they help one work better. No wonder "work" has become a four-letter word for the Now Generation.

Some writers point to the Bible as the source of the idea that God's intention for man is hard, unsatisfying work. The Garden of Eden is described as an idyllic place where man's needs were fulfilled without work. They haven't read the story! Man's expulsion from Eden (Genesis 3) did result in man working by the sweat of his brow with unrewarding earth. What is overlooked in this symbolic story is the profound insight that such *meaningless* work, such drudgery, was the result of man's disobedience. *Before* his expulsion, man was pictured as working ("The Lord God took the man and put him in the Garden of Eden to till it and take care of it"), but then it was with a sense of satisfaction and purpose. This was God's original intention for man.

Work in the Scheme of Things

Now we must note that work is just one facet of life, and that work must be combined with many other activities if life is to be satisfying. In his excellent book, *The Time of Our Lives: The Ethics of Common Sense*, Mortimer Adler puts work in a better perspective. He suggests that there are five uses of time, all of which are needed for the "good life."

The first is that set of activities which are necessary for survival—sleeping, eating, bathing, etc. These are compulsory, if we want to live at all. As a rough guess, such activities consume about one-third of our life. Of course, the *way* we satisfy these needs can be a source of pleasure, companionship, and delight, too.

The second kind of activity is that which is economically

necessary. Adler calls this "subsistence-work," and it is compulsory for all of us who do not have access to wealth. This, too, takes about one-third of our life. "Subsistence-work" can be unmitigated drudgery or deeply pleasurable. It can be undertaken solely for the money involved, or it can be the kind of job worth undertaking even if one did not have to earn a living. Or somewhere in between.

For most people, these first two activities are something they *must* do to stay alive. We now look at three activities we *can* do to enrich life.

The distinguishing characteristic of "play" lies in its being neither necessary nor useful. It serves no special purpose, produces no result beyond pleasure. Play can be spontaneous, but it frequently, as in games, proceeds according to rules accepted by the players. Its pleasures cease when we stop playing. Many people have transformed play into work, as when grimly compelling achievement or a serious, determined performance contaminates their "play." Some have professionalized it into work.

Fourthly, there is "idling," doing nothing, or as little as possible. Sunbathing is a good example, unless you combine it with getting a date; then it may become work!

There is at least one other form of human activity that is crucial. Unlike sleep and subsistence-work, it is not compulsory. Unlike play and idling, it is useful activity, with the purpose of producing a lasting result. It aims at personal and general human improvement; it is self-creative because it involves personal growth and enrichment, whatever the activity involved. Adler calls it "leisure" or "leisuring." Leisuring, or "leisure-work" is not merely something we do with the time left after compulsory activities. "Leisure-work" may be pleasurable; it usually is. But that is not its main point. It always involves learning and serious endeavor. It may seem strange that love and friendship are among the chief areas of "leisure-work," but they are. But it should be remembered that you seldom succeed in love or friendship unless you really work at it (every good marriage must be cultivated) and learn from it in the process.

I shall not go further into Adler's sophisticated analysis of the five parts of life, except to say two things that are important for us here. First, the author suggests a test question: Assuming that you wanted to make a good life for yourself and *did not have to think about earning a living* (subsistence-work), and assuming that your life was unaffected by good or bad fortune, how would you spend the time at your disposal? Think about that for a while.

Secondly, Adler suggests that one can never do too much leisuring, because leisuring is directed toward full development and creativity. He concludes that if one has a choice of jobs, one should avoid pure subsistence-work and try to take a job that pays a living wage but which involves as much leisure-work as possible, a job that does more for you and other human beings. Only a man who does not know the difference between living and living well would choose a job of drudgery in order to earn a very large income. Common sense dictates, says Adler, that it would be better to choose a job that pays less but is more self-rewarding.

SUCCESS VS. PLEASURE IN WORK

Unfortunately, few of us live by the common sense advocated by Adler. We are not that reasonable. We are driven by many needs, some irrational, some self-destructive. Basically, we all want happiness, although we cannot find it if we seek it directly. It is assumed, in our society and in many others, that if one can be a "success" in his field, can make a name for himself, happiness will be his. The one who fails is supposed to be condemned either to unhappiness or to a continuing struggle to reach that magical state of "success." Is success simply recognition for work? I don't think so. Of course, everyone wants recognition for what he does well. I am enjoying writing this book and hope that when it is published, its readers will like it and get something from it. I believe that is a worthwhile goal, worth postponing other pleasure for a time. But simply having a book published and appreciated by its readers is not regarded as "success" by the public. A book must reach the best seller lists; it must climb to the top. Then the author has it made.

Competitive success means a desire to elevate oneself above one's fellows. One's sense of worth depends upon standing out, even standing *above* others. Such a desire seems to begin early in childhood. No one ever is told that he is good enough as he is. It is assumed that this would lead to laziness, apathy, and a lack of desire for growth or accomplishment. How many parents are afraid to praise their children for anything they do well?

We sometimes assume this drive for superiority and success is distinctly American, indeed, distinctly modern. Not so. It has been found in every culture, in every era, though perhaps not to the same extent. If you will stop now, pick up a modern version of the New Testament, and read Mark 9, you will see clearly how these motives were at work among the disciples as they did the "work of the Lord." It's a penetrating case study. Jesus took the three favored disciples up to the mountain where something mysterious happened; they later called it "transfiguration." They did not understand it, but what frightened them most was Jesus' comment, which he had made earlier, that he would be killed if he continued in his course. Consider the effect upon the disciples. They had left their regular jobs (fishing, tax collecting, etc.), and they already were being laughed at for taking up their new "work" with this itinerant rabbi. If he died, what could they do but return home humiliated? Furthermore, if the Master were to be killed, what about their own safety?

Clearly, the disciples were anxious when they came down the hill to join the other disciples, who were not doing so well, either. Thinking themselves fully prepared to carry on Jesus' ministry, they had tried to heal an epileptic boy and had failed.

What a blow to their self-esteem! But notice what happened next. Jesus healed the boy, and told the disciples why they had failed; then they all began their journey through Galilee. As they came to Capernaum, Jesus asked them what they had been talking about as they walked along. They were silent, because they actually had been discussing who among them was the greatest (Mark 9:34). Having lost their inner security and direction, the men of this close-knit group *began to compete with one another*, to make their place in the world secure, to discover to whom they were superior.

The Bible tells us that Jesus responded by placing a child in their midst. Still the disciples needed to feel one-up on someone, so they continued to seek self-elevation.

"John said to him, 'Master, we saw a man driving out devils in your name, and as he was not one of *us*, we tried to stop him.' (In other words, if he's not in *our* group, the in-group, Lord, he can't do anything good. We are superior.) But Jesus said, 'Do not stop him . . . For he who is not against us is on our side . . .'" (Mark 9:38–40. New English Bible). As can be seen, the need to succeed in competition, the need for superiority is not new. The desire for self-elevation surfaces whenever we feel insecure and anxious, whenever we feel inferior or inadequate.

If such motives control us in our work, however, they will defeat the very happiness we hope to find. Such motives never bring a lasting sense of satisfaction and inner peace. For one thing, we are highly vulnerable to anyone who might surpass us. We constantly compare ourselves with others. If others rise in rank or position, our self-esteem takes a nosedive. Our sense of self-worth goes up and down like a yo-yo, depending upon where we stand compared with others. The sensation of success is followed by the torture of anticipated failure. Even when a goal is achieved, it usually does not give us the hoped-for good feeling, the sense of liberation. The drive for self-elevation is insatiable. What is worse, the values of "winning" infiltrate all of life, so that we judge not only ourselves but our parents, children, wife and friends by their place in the hierarchy of success.

The competitive person is saturated with *envy*, which the church fathers called, not without good reason, one of the seven deadly sins. Wishing we had what someone else has is one of the most potent sources of unhappiness. Envy is nourished by comparing ourselves with others. Instead of finding pleasure in what we have, we are hurt by envy of what others have. It leads us either to try to copy the envied one, or to gossip hatefully about him. Envy leads us to belittle what we admire but can't have.

But—and this is important—you can admire what another person has achieved without envying him if *you* have your *own* goals for life, and if you understand God's will for *you*. Competitive success does not necessarily cure envy because there always will be someone more successful than you. You can escape envy only by enjoying the pleasures that do come your way, by finding enjoyment in your work, by refusing to compare yourself or your lot, with those you imagine, often falsely, to be more fortunate than you. Another's life often looks more interesting when you don't have to live it.

Let me offer some questions to test the degree to which you may be driven by a neurotic need for competitive success:

1. Do you constantly measure yourself against others, even others who do not share your goals or life situation?

2. Deep down, do you really want to be best of all or better than others in what you do? Even when others say you have accomplished something worthwhile, do you feel disappointed or depressed when you realize that someone can do it better than you?

3. Do you feel as if the success of another person is a failure for you? Is it harder for you to have a friend tell you of a victory or accomplishment than to tell you his troubles? Do you feel angry or depressed when someone you know achieves prominence or is recognized for a job he did?

4. Do you always feel as if you should have done something better? Do you scold yourself for not being perfect, for making mistakes? Do you feel depressed and "no good" about your mistakes?

5. Do you, in your most honest moments, feel resentment and bitterness that anyone is more intelligent, more attractive, more influential, more popular than you?

6. Do you sometimes feel inhibited in even trying to set or reach a goal? Would you rather withdraw than to risk failure?

If your answer to any two of these questions is "yes", you are to some extent in the grasp of an idealized image of success. When work gets wrapped up in this kind of self-demand, it frequently is drained of its pleasure. It is no fun to be always in a contest. Is this what people are for?

There's Another Way

The desire for self-elevation is not necessary for growth, accomplishment and happiness. There is another motivation, less acknowledged, but much more reliable and not as costly to the person and to society. It is the desire to be *useful* and to do something that is *necessary* for the well-being of others. The push behind such a desire is enthusiasm for an activity, love, interest, and the enjoyment of living, in contrast to the motivation for competitive success which is lust for glory, power, and self-elevation.

The desire to be useful never can be frustrated. It always is related to what one *can* do and enjoys doing. Whatever life might have in store, something can be done about it. While there never is a perfect solution, you always can work to improve the situation. You no longer fear making mistakes; you grow in the courage to live with imperfection. Doing what you can do and what you enjoy doing does not require comparing yourself with others. You invest the talents you have, sure of your own value because God gave you *some* talent, *some* way of being useful.

Of course, you may wish to be a "helper," to discard the lures of success and money, and still find yourself drawn only to those prestige positions which sometimes are far from where the action is. At least for part of your career, I wish that more of you young people would work as policemen, as prison guards, and at other kinds of jobs where you will be able to exert unmeasured influence at the deep levels of life where it is hurting. Those of you who have read Ken Kesey's *One Flew Over the Cuckoo's Nest* or Hannah Green's *I Never Promised You a Rose Garden* know the crucial importance of a mental hospital's ward attendants or psychiatric aids in the lives of the emotionally disturbed.

You may be disappointed if things do not turn out as well as you had hoped with some work, but you will not be defeated or plunged into a feeling of worthlessness. What you did may have been wrong, stupid, or mistaken, but this does not mean that *you* are stupid or a failure. One of the most fascinating aspects of man's nature—one he does not share with the lower animals—is his ability to carry on internal dialogues with himself. He talks to himself about his experiences. *What he tells himself* is crucial to his well-being. Others can make comments about him, but unless he says the same things to himself, the words will have little effect on him. A person who has realized his worth to God and himself is inwardly free. Everybody likes approval, but the free man does not depend on it.

Many people have grown up with the heresy that if work is Christian or a calling from God, it must be unpleasant. I worked with a college student who thoroughly enjoyed working with youngsters and was considering a job as a YMCA secretary. But he found it difficult to think of it as his life's work because it was so much fun. (His father had worked all his life, at something he hated with a passionate sense of grim duty and this attitude had rubbed off on his son.) The best way to find happiness in work is to discover your interests and then find what fits your talents. Pleasure comes when you are totally committed, mind and body, to an activity you enjoy and you know is useful. John R. Mott, that great Christian teacher of half a century ago, was asked what constituted a Christian vocation, or "calling": "A need known and capacity to meet that need; that constitutes a call."

All of us must do some hard thinking about what is useful and necessary in our world of artificially-induced consumer needs and luxuries when half the world is in poverty and oppression. Sam Keen, a young theologian, talks about force-feeding the insatiable consumer with what blocks his arteries: cars and cholesterol. The result is a stoppage of real life by the traffic jam and the heart attack. For those drawn by the figure of Jesus, the best clue as to what is necessary and useful comes in his words in Luke:

"He stood up to read the lesson and was handed the scroll of the prophet Isaiah. He opened the scroll and found the passage which says,
'The spirit of the Lord is upon me because he has anointed me; he has sent me to announce good news to the poor,
to proclaim release for prisoners and recovery of sight for the blind;
to let the broken victims go free,
to proclaim the year of the Lord's favour.'
He rolled up the scroll, gave it back to the attendant, and sat down; and all eyes in the synogogue were fixed on him. He began to speak: 'Today,' he said, 'in your very hearing this text has come true'." (Luke 4:17–21, New English Bible).

The first member of the Now Generation! Such work begins now, and no one is ever out of a job with this commission. Is this what people are for? To help others recover their full humanity, to give them release, freedom? If such is our work, "instant competency" is out of the question since we always will be striving to hone our tools, including ourselves. That needs discipline; it sometimes means the delay of immediate gratification so that we can bring more skill to situations of need. In this kind of freedom, discipline means still greater freedom to act effectively. It means placing certain values upon our various interests.

If I am to find a new reality, I must tie together the next few months or years in unified action. My minor decisions—play, idling, etc.—will be made in terms of my long-range purposes or goals. Freedom is our power to *bind time*, our power to knit together succeeding moments, even years, by means of a dominant purpose. Because of this, as the future unfolds we become progressively free as we practice our skills to do what we could not do before. Our options increase with our joy in using those skills.

My hunch is that many young people are not willing either to wait or to sacrifice to become competent, or skilled, because they don't have anything they really want to do. They have lost their sense of wonder; they cannot think of anything that fascinates them. They have not decided what they want their lives to say.

4.

Love or Instant Intimacy?

Young people hunger deeply for closeness, for intimacy. The rest of us do, too, for that matter. But there is an urgency about the search of the young. They are the children of the "Lonely Crowd." Their elders, steeped in habits, social roles, responsibilities, have settled for less than youth will.

Openness and closeness to people, to nature, to God all are cherished. Whatever gets in between experience and life tends to be tossed aside. Young people are tired of hearsay, tired of looking through the opaque windows of someone else's stained-glass experience, tired of prepackaged answers. They want to be immediately aware, even though they are not sure of just what it is they will find. Simon and Garfunkel's "Cloudy" beautifully portrays shifting colors, the rushing feelings, the giant ink-blot of the sky, the search for life's meaning.

Young people want to know themselves, nature and God, first hand, not through what they feel is their elders' distorted lenses. They want to be "in touch." In a wordy world, they've discovered that "coming to their senses" is one way to know themselves. What children sense instinctively, and psychotherapists have learned by research, young people have been rediscovering: that to the extent that you feel your body to be alive and real, you feel yourself to be alive and real. One has but to observe the youth scene to discover that the pleasure of being fully alive comes through breathing, and movement, and feeling. We are, indeed, in a "feeling revolution," as well as a social revolution.

Young people want intimacy with nature. Susanne Langer wrote in her *Philosophy in a New Key:*

> "We have put many stages of artifice and device, of manufacture and alteration, between ourselves and the rest of nature. The ordinary city dweller . . . does not know the sunrise and rarely notices when the sun sets; ask him in what phase the moon is in, or when the tide in the harbor is high, . . . and likely as not he cannot answer you. Seedtime and harvest are nothing to him. If he has never witnessed an earthquake, a great flood, or a hurricane, he probably does not feel the power of nature as a reality surrounding his life at all . . ." *

The ecological revolution is changing that. And young people, perhaps as never before in an urban culture, are in touch with the delicate balance of natural forces in our world.

No second-hand religion will do for them, either. Rufus Jones, the Quaker, used to say that if our only experience with a sunset was through descriptions passed down to us from earlier generations, we would be poor, indeed, and would not be convinced of its reality. The church has been miserably deficient in providing opportunities for religious experiences which are compellingly real. Instead, a "ballet of bloodless concepts" or a recital of dry history often pass for Christianity. The zeal of young people for direct experience demands bread instead of the stones that their fathers in the faith often have offered them. They want a faith that is living, throbbing, pulsing with life and freedom. They are resistant to the bull-dozer approach of certain religionists, their moral exhortations and their psychological weapons designed to increase conscious-

* Susanne K. Langer, *Philosophy in a New Key.* Boston: Harvard University Press, 1953, p. 278.

ness of guilt. Young people are tired of having their noses rubbed in their errors. Contrast this kind of manipulation with Jesus' attitude of respect and humility as he said, "Behold, I stand at the door and knock. If any man hears my voice and opens the door, I will come in. . . ." Young people want reality and personal freedom in religion.

Most of all, this new generation wants genuine intimacy with men and women. It is disillusioned with token relationships. Closeness and self-disclosure frighten many, but increasing numbers are willing to live in contact with others without running away. It's risky, it's scary, they admit, but it's better than isolation. Who wants to live life as a spectator? Only those who have learned to handle life's inevitable anxiety by *avoidance*, by running away. Some stay away from others because they expect catastrophic things to happen. "People won't like me." "I might do something foolish." These ballooning fantasies prevent a person from taking the normal risks of contact with others. Only courage and common sense can shrink such fantasies. We do not free ourselves from something by avoiding it, but only by living through it.

More and more, the stress on organizational life is countered by the demand of young people for honesty and openness that can be met, if at all, in extremely close relationships. And in such relationships, the focus is upon the release of feelings, upon unashamed encounter with the other person. One wonders if these relationships can bear the weight of the high romantic expectations held for them, since there is little preparation for the antagonisms which arise in the very closeness that is demanded.

The new generation recognizes that, both in and out of marriage, people don't need each other anymore to work a farm, to spin yarn, even to wash dishes. The bonds of a relationship exist not for survival but for affection and understanding. Once a husband and wife may have loved each other because they needed each other. Now the situation has changed. They need each other because they love each other.

INSTANT INTIMACY

The desire to squeeze a lifetime into a day has led many young people into a search for instant emotional and physical contact. Some will not wait for relationships to ripen naturally. There is no time for introductions, for getting acquainted, for getting used to one another. There is a widely held belief that real things happen spontaneously, quickly, and that people ought to be completely open to each other immediately.

Item: "I notice you're a Capricorn—we'll groove."

Item: Advertisement: "Computer Dating Saves Time and Disappointment."

Item: At a college party, a boy approaches an attractive girl. "How about going to bed with me? This party is a drag." "But I've just met you!" "What better way to get acquainted?"

Item: At the first session of a university encounter group, a veteran "grouper" pushes a newcomer: "I'm fed up with you for refusing to level with us. Why don't you admit you're here because you're bored with your husband and looking for a boy friend?" (Message: share your secret with us right now).

Item: "Man, have I got good vibes from you!"

Item: Nude marathons and communal baths are sweeping the United States as a new way (for middle-agers, mostly) to escape from boredom and "be open" to each other. I understand that the only thing participants are reluctant to reveal at such well-attended events is their incomes. The fig leaf still clings to the wallet!

Privacy, reserve, formalities seem to be on their way out. Those not willing to play the game of "instant intimacy" are accused of being up-tight. It is contact, not love, which is important to many now. Since they are convinced they can find only moments of positive experience, they think they have to get with it.

A young person may work fast, but usually only with someone who has similar values. It doesn't take long to discover whether you're on the same wave length. One observer of the thousands of young people traveling to Europe in the summer (two of every five United States citizens granted a passport in 1969 were under 30) noted how easily hippie-type couples found each other. From whatever country they came, they seemed to be joined together by rock music, anti-Establishment movies, marijuana, and the "V" salute for peace. Instant, if not linguistic, rapport is apparent. Great numbers of "travel marriages" spring up and many young people, upon returning home, remember among other things "a shabby room, a groovy chick, and a warm feeling," reported *Newsweek*, in its August 10, 1970, issue. Commitment is limited to hours or days—and then it's over.

In instant intimacy there is no vision of a future together, and each person feels free to end the relationship whenever he or she wishes. It might seem that such relationships are honest and open, but the opposite often is true. Couples who travel or live together for a short time like to think that they do so for more than sexual convenience. Therefore, they often convince themselves that they have achieved a good, intimate relationship. The first disagreement or argument, the first bout of boredom reveals how fragile it really is, and this leads to "splitting" and the search for a new partner.

Contrast instant intimacy, usually characterized by a lustful sexuality, with the intimacy of a good marriage. The deep sharing of the whole self with another requires trust and common experience. It is unlikely to develop between two people who have serious reservations as to how long they will stay together. When people have no serious commitment to each other, they are unwilling to risk being open with one another. That's why *fidelity* is so crucial to a fulfilling relationship.

Instant intimacy often is characterized by pretense and hypocrisy. The desire for transparency and openness is supposed to eliminate hypocrisy. But there are *two* kinds of hypocrisy. Young people see that, in their Victorian elders, hypocrisy takes the form of acting respectably ("good taste") while hiding true feelings behind a mask, and they rightly condemn this. What often is overlooked, however, is that many young people engage in a kind of "reverse hypocrisy"—*seeming* to be more in favor of current behavior than they really are. One must never seem to dislike the latest music, to disagree with the most avant garde idea, or the most extreme of the "free" spirits. A person actually may have deep, positive convictions about love, marriage, and fidelity but be afraid to reveal them. Many a young person has confessed *guilt* about such hangups! Such duplicity takes as high a psychological toll as does the hypocrisy of their elders.

I have noticed that student propaganda about the popularity of sexual experience outruns the facts. "But everyone does it —or do they?" asks Evelyn Duvall in her honest little book, *Why Wait Till Marriage?* After examining all the major scientific studies of student sexual behavior she concludes that by the time they are 21, perhaps half of the men and one-fourth of the women college students have had sexual experience. Joseph Katz, in his impressive four-year study of California university students (where sexual behavior is supposed to be the weathervane for the nation), found through use of an anonymous questionnaire that 60 per cent of Stanford University men and 61 per cent of University of California men said they had had no sexual intercourse up to the middle of their junior year. Sixty-two per cent of the Stanford women and 72 per cent of the University of California women said the same. Furthermore, sex received a rather low grade when compared to other factors, such as careers, love and affection, personal identity, and finding time for thinking and reflection. Increasing numbers of these students (up to one-half of the men) were willing to wait to marry until they were over 25 years of age.

I have a hunch that bored middle-agers, raised by a Victorian code, are more attracted to instant intimacy than are the young people. Sexual contacts on business trips, in week-end "encounter" groups and at conventions, and the "urge to orge" in respectable suburbs, are the signs of libertine society in middle America. Youth are looking for something deeper than a spasm of clandestine sexuality born of a dull, habitual life.

How Can Anything That Feels So Good Be So Bad?

There's nothing bad about sexual urges. After all, they are God's idea. But the meaning and enjoyment of sex depends on the relationship. Sex is a vehicle for many intentions. "Sex is sex is sex," say some, remembering Gertrude Stein's definition of a rose. If it were only that simple! Instead, a *relationship* is involved which determines the meaning, sometimes even the intensity of the sexual experience. Unfortunately, our language doesn't reflect the many faces of sex. Eskimos have 15 words describing different kinds of snow; Arabs can distinguish at least seven varieties of sand. When your life depends upon something, you learn to make distinctions. Even though Western culture is saturated by sexual stimuli, we have scarcely made a start on a vocabulary which would describe the meaning of sex in different relationships and circumstances.

In spite of our illiteracy about this important area of our lives, there are some distinctions that still come through in our poverty-stricken language. Stop now, and think of all the three, four, and five-letter words meaning sexual intercourse that you know. Isn't it interesting that most of these words connote something one person *does to* another person? They seem to have taken on an aggressive meaning. They are not concerned with mutuality of desire and experience, as is the word "*inter*course." Dr. Karl Menninger, the well-known psychiatrist, warned decades ago that the blending of hostile feelings with sexual feelings is a near-fatal combination in human relationships. Radical youth express violent hostility largely with references to the sex act, as in "F— you!" This expletive really is a term of contempt for another person who is used for one's own purposes and then discarded as of no value whatsoever.

Sex not only is used to express hostility but for other motives, too. What I said in another place describes some of them:

"Christianity affirms that coitus finds its basic meaning in a truly *personal relationship*. This kind of love depends upon the ability to give and receive the kind of affection and care which brings out the potentialities of the partner. Yet many episodes are not a part of a personal relationship. It is not love but *lust* which motivates the act. *Lust is impersonal sexuality*, pleasure or security sought for its own sake . . . Many diverse motives are channeled into the sex act. The girl who reports, 'I'm so hungry for love that if a boy shows me even a little tenderness, there is nothing I will not do for him,' may be seeking affectional security. The fraternity or military man who is compulsively building up his sex record may be seeking status with his brothers and attempting to prove his own masculinity about which he has doubts." *

Today, many couples "couple" just for the release of tension and for the physical pleasure that comes from the sex act, without any thought of a sustained or even a personal relationship. They may simply lust after each other. It is the body that counts, not the person. Some are in training to be sexual athletes on both the men's and women's teams. This is the answer to the question: Does sex need love? Of course not. Anyone can "sex"; far fewer will learn to love. No one who has seen "M.A.S.H." can doubt that you can have sex purely as recreation, without any attachment whatsoever to the partner. It is my impression that sex without a genuine relationship seldom if ever leads to love, while love almost always leads to a desire to express oneself sexually with one's partner.

* Roy W. Fairchild, *Christians in Families*. Covenant Life Curriculum. Richmond: John Knox Press, 1964, pp. 80–81.

What is communicated *through* sexual behavior is never determined by the sex act itself.

Many people take the simplistic point of view that *any* sex outside of marriage is wrong and that *any* sex inside of marriage is right. They completely miss the fact that sex can carry so many messages. Sex relations are another form of human relations. Within marriage, sex can be exploitive, legalized prostitution, a bartering for services rendered, and dull habit. Just because sex is expressed within marriage doesn't necessarily mean its basic meaning is fulfilled, the growth of persons together is guaranteed. In some ways I am more concerned these days about "married unlove" than about "unmarried love." But this discussion depends on the meaning of love, which we'll get into shortly.

Sex treated like a drink of water or a good sneeze separates the body and mind in a dualism that is fatal to the health of the person and of society, not to mention a valid understanding of Christianity. The "coupling" of two bodies is easy; the union of two persons is a very difficult but rewarding achievement. Sex, in Christian understanding, is both a reflection of and a means to that union. It is a gift for both expressing and for nourishing love. In this context, sex cannot be hit-and-run and in a hurry. It involves "knowing" (the biblical term for intercourse) a person at a deep level in all aspects of life— the sharing of dreams, tastes, interests, fears from the past, hopes for the future. This takes more time, more trust, more care and more communication than simply going to bed with each other. I never will forget Lester Kirkendall's report of his interview of a college man during Kirkendall's survey of student sexual activity. After the man had reported sexual intercourse with a coed, Kirkendall asked, "Did the girl experience an orgasm?" The student replied, "I really don't know—it would have been embarrassing to ask her. I didn't know her well enough."

Sex may be greatly overrated as "the way to get acquainted." It may be fun, it may not be. How often today one hears the comment, "We went to bed but it wasn't so good." In any event, too-early sexual experience often leads to such a preoccupation with bodily contact that one really cannot come to know the other person very well. Listening to one another, growing closer and more tender, sharing secrets and dreams— all this can be shoved aside by an obsession with sex. Really, sex is only a *part* of life. It often is thought of as the "peak experience" of existence; yet people neglect the fact that, after the honeymoon, direct sexual expression takes only about 10 per cent of one's time in marriage. What are you going to do with the other 90 per cent? No wonder so many young marriages fail. Married love is more than a bedtime story.

It might seem incredible to those of you reading this book, but some experts in the personality sciences are saying that sex as we now think of it may soon be dead! We've heard of the "death of God" movement, but *sex*? How can such a vital, exciting function die? Rollo May, whose book *Love and Will* is a "must" for any student of human relations today, maintains that with the increased availability of sexual experience to anyone who wants it outside of marriage, sex has become, for many, machine-like and boring. Unrestrained sexual freedom has produced not more pleasure but a detached, empty compulsion without feeling and monotonously cheerless. "The more sex the merrier" has not led to more spontaneity but to a mechanistic attitude toward love-making, enhanced, of course, by the countless "how-to-do-it" books now on every newsstand.

Art Hoppe, *San Francisco Chronicle* columnist, made this memorable point in an article entitled: "Keep Sex Dirty." In a fantasy account of the future, he portrays a time when all restraints on unlimited sex are finally broken down:

"Psychologists, sociologists and philosophers were ecstatic. 'At last,' they said, 'mankind has rid himself of his age-old fears and complexes about sex. At last he will have the same healthy attitudes toward sex as he has toward, say, jogging.'

And they proved to be absolutely right. The public came to look on sex precisely as it had looked upon jogging. The effects were disastrous.

"First hit were the foreign art films. Who wanted to watch 143 minutes of uninterrupted jogging? . . . Topless reviews went bust. Bottomless reviews hit bottom . . . And the unemployment rate on Madison Avenue, where voyeurism had been the prime stock in trade, reached 67.3 percent. The economy tottered.

"Worst of all, precisely the same proportion of the public now practiced sex as had practiced jogging—.08 per cent. . . . The future of the human race hung in the balance.

"It was saved by the DAR which . . . launched a massive Dirty Sex Drive under the slogan: 'Cherish the Heritage of our Forefathers—Make Sex Dirty Again.' 'Sex is illicit?' cried the ladies, a blush on the cheeks. 'Sex is dirty?' cried the gentlemen, a gleam in their eye. Once again, adultery flourished, love nests were bared, voyeurism thrived, the economy prospered, and humanity survived."

For many, engaging in sex is more like learning acrobatics. This can be seen in the drop-of-a-hat episodes in "Hair." A funny thing happened on the way to complete sex freedom. The more it declared its freedom from the old Victorian "shoulds," the more sex *outside* a committed relationship *became* a "must"! In countless subtle ways, a contemporary youth is made to feel guilty for "saving sex for marriage," or for thinking of it as anything more than temporary fun or tension-release. When sex becomes, as it has for so many, simply repeated seductions to avoid despair (and to avoid the problems of creating a good life for the people of the world), we can see that sex is in danger of dying. Sex without passion and commitment and caring becomes, at last, just plain boring and an escape from life.

When people say, "Why wait? You can have it all now," I want to say, "That depends on what you want."

Christianity's insistence on fidelity as an important ingredient of the sexual relationship did not come from ancient lawgivers who wanted to spoil the fun of the young. When the Master came that we might have "abundant life," that included sex. Seward Hiltner claims that casual sex cannot give life real intensity and pleasure, not only for the body but for the whole person.

"Intensity is desirable from each of the relevant perspectives: biologically, in the intense pleasure of the encounter and the orgasm; psychologically, in the discovery of unsuspected depths in the self; socially, in the depth of discovery of another; ethically, in the integration of fulfillment and responsibility and theologically, in the deepening sense of the mystery." *

It all depends on what you want. If you want depth and meaning, instant intimacy does not deliver.

ANOTHER FOUR LETTER WORD: LOVE

No word in the English language carries more misleading meanings. When we say a person loves tennis, loves cokes, loves his car, loves Simon and Garfunkel, loves his wife, we may mean he is *attached* in some way to all of them but beyond that, the word becomes distorted beyond understanding. Both caring and hatred can be expressed by the word "love." "I love you" can mean genuine affection or cruel domination, because who can protest something done "because I love you." As we use the term "love," it can mean anything or nothing.

The Greeks had at least four words for love. First, there is *epithemia*, or sheer physical desire or lust. Second, there is *eros* (from which our adjective, "erotic," comes). This suggests a passionate attraction to that which is good, true and beautiful. It is a longing, a desire for what is worth possessing. *Eros* may

* Seward Hiltner, *Sex and the Christian Life*. New York: Association Press, 1957, pp. 86–87.

include sex, but sex without passion, for the release of tension or for recreation only, is not *eros.* A third word is *philia,* which refers basically to friendship or brotherly love. It is comradely, warm, affectionate, but confined to those who are near and dear to you. *Agape'* is self-giving love which is not based primarily on emotion. It is action taken on behalf of others—friends *and* enemies. It is undertaken to foster the well-being and growth of the person loved. *Agape'* is characteristic of God's action. *Agape'* is what St. Paul speaks of in his first letter to the Corinthians:

"Love is patient; love is kind and envies no one. Love is never boastful, nor conceited, nor rude; never selfish, not quick to take offense. Love keeps no score of wrongs; does not gloat over other men's sins, but delights in the truth. There is nothing love cannot face; there is no limit to its faith, its hope, and its endurance" (I Corinthians 13:4–7).

Every love between a man and a woman is a blending, in varying proportions, of these kinds of love. Research conducted on couples who are contented with their marriages and who have reared apparently happy children reveals that the words they most often use to describe their marriages are *companionship* and *respect.* These are elements of *philia.* An enduring, happy marriage depends heavily upon both *liking* each other, not chiefly on romantic passion. But it is clear that *agapé* and *eros* cannot be absent. A good marriage demands that a person love his neighbor as himself. (Martin Luther said one's mate is one's nearest neighbor). One does not love "the neighbor" *instead* of oneself. It is a balance of self-seeking and self-giving. The art of loving in a home is discovering how to fill one's own needs and the needs of the family at the same time. This is no easy job, especially when those needs seem to clash.

Fortunately, one does not always have to feel pleasant toward the other in order to love, in the Christian sense. *Love is something you do.* One of the best practical tests of a love relationship comes to us from the noted psychiatrist, the late

Harry Stack Sullivan: *"When the satisfaction or the security of another person becomes as significant as is one's own satisfaction or security, then a state of love exists."* * It is well to ponder the meaning of Christian *agape'* and Sullivan's definition of love as we confront the feeling revolution which is upon us. The language of love can conceal as well as reveal; feelings can mislead as well as give a clue to truth. Behavior is a more reliable test.

A maturing love differs from instant intimacy in three important respects: it needs fig-leaves, it needs fidelity, and it needs caring in order to keep it vital.

Love needs fig-leaves. What do I mean? I mean that I do not reveal everything to everybody. In his deepest self everyone is a mystery, even to himself at times. In one sense, I am ultimately alone. I have my own way of seeing, of feeling, of thinking. No one can share directly my memories, my passions, my fears. Only I live inside my skin. If this were not so, we would not have to communicate, to use words, symbols, and gestures as bridges to the lives of others. Everyone who loves is driven by the double necessity of listening and talking, of revealing and discovering, for it is the authentic mark of love to know and be known. Simon and Garfunkel have picked up the sadness of our day in "The Sound of Silence," which tells of "people talking without speaking; people hearing without listening." Even when we intend to share ourselves, when we decide not to conceal, our fondest gestures seem to fall short of what we would say by them. Still, we say what we can, we unveil sacred things, even silly and guilty things, to trustful eyes and depend upon another's belief in our words and gestures. You can only know me if I want you to know me. In love, such self-disclosure does take place; otherwise, we live not with real persons but with images of them created in our imagination. We endanger love when we build up in our

* Harry Stack Sullivan, *Conceptions of Modern Psychiatry.* New York: W. W. Norton & Co., 1953, pp. 42–43.

own minds a fictional world which we believe the loved one inhabits. But the real point is that we do not disclose ourselves to everyone—only to those we trust.

This is what I mean by "fig leaves." The story of Adam and Eve is the story of Everyman. Many modern utopian dreams call for us to reveal ourselves to everyone. The Bible is more realistic. Its authors were well aware that there would be those who would take advantage of us, as well as those who would protect us, warm us, love us. Jesus cautioned us in an unforgettable way because of the seeming abrasiveness of his words: "Do not throw your pearls before swine!" That is, do not give what is precious to you to those who cannot appreciate its value. And what is more precious than the secret? He who has your secret has potential power over you. The art of getting ahead in the world, one cynic has said, depends "not on *what* you know, not on *who* you know, but on *what* you have on who you know."

To be open and frank with the ones you love calls for a certain *reserve* with others. I know this statement is heresy to many in the sensitivity group movement, but I am convinced of its wisdom. We are *selective* in our relationships; with those we trust we are open; with those we do not yet trust, we are reticent. In fact, there is even a need for reticence within love and friendship. There must be "spaces in our togetherness." We respect another's right to solitude, to privacy. We give those we love full right to their own inner life until they choose to reveal it. Real human love has both closeness and distance within it.

Love needs fidelity. Man has been defined as the one being who can make and keep promises. That is, he projects himself into the future and faithfully pledges that an intention experienced now will be held to in that future. Erik Erikson, the well-known psychoanalyst, maintains that genuine intimacy depends upon the ability to make and abide by commitments. Commitments are relative: some are for hours, some for weeks, some for a lifetime. One can immediately

question seriously Christianity's emphasis on lifelong commitment to one marriage partner "until death do us part."
What if one's feelings change? What if the relationship "dies?"
There is enough evidence of dead marriages, in which the
partners live as cell-mates, to prompt this question. What
kind of life does marriage offer when only its form is left, without any of the vitality it had in the beginning?

Young people don't want to be caught in that trap. They
sometimes begin to feel that *any* commitment, any vow of
steadfastness and fidelity, will rob a relationship of its reality.
Some young people set up households which are supposed to
be tied together by interest, love, and intimacy alone. If those
feelings evaporate, the people involved end the relationship
without legal hassles. This, undoubtedly, is a more honest situation than many marriages with which we are acquainted.
Many young people, insisting on honesty, would like to change
the wedding vows from "as long as we both shall live" to "as
long as we both shall *love*"; from "till death do us part" to
"till we get bored with each other"; from "forsaking all others" to "until someone who will make me really happy comes
along."

A love relationship, however, needs *both* genuine feeling for
each other and fidelity. One does not have to choose between
uncommitted hippie-type love and committed Victorian dull-
ness. Hippie love does contain the ingredients of immediacy,
spontaneity, and emotional honesty of the moment. But love
needs to be steadfast and enduring, too. It needs a strong will
to make it. Love grows through the encounter of lovers with
each other, sometimes in conflict, and the willingness to learn
from such friction over a period of time. Couples who live together with no anticipation of permanency are always taking
their emotional temperatures. When life becomes unpleasant,
they withdraw from it. They lack the tolerance of frustration
which helps them face and work through the inevitable problems in any relationship, such as anger and aggressiveness.

Conflict is also a part of genuine intimacy. Is real openness likely to develop between a couple who have serious reservations as to how long they will stay together? When we give all our loyalty to someone who counts on us and upon whom we can count, we are willing to become vulnerable to each other and, through such open and honest sharing, to grow and change. Periodic doses of instant intimacy simply do not substitute for an enduring relationship in which there is warmth, companionship, sexual delight and joy, as well as pain, discipline, and frustration. Fidelity frees one to become more imaginative in his marriage.

In his *Art of Living* Andre Maurois said, "I bind myself for life; I have chosen; from now on my aim will be not to search for someone who will please me, but to please the one I have chosen." * If a loving relationship in marriage is anything, it is a costly achievement, a persisting and cheerful effort, and an artful and exciting creation. And that takes time, and imagination, and care—and fidelity alone is not enough. We must learn to be *creatively* faithful, giving ourselves without reservation, extending the kind of embracing warmth that allows each person in the partnership to flourish. Such steadfastness is its own reward.

Monogamous marriage, as a form of fidelity, is in an ambiguous situation today. When one views the divorce statistics (in California there are about six divorces for every 10 marriages), one could conclude that marriage is on its way out. But that is not true. Marriage is so popular that more than 80 per cent of those divorced marry again, some as soon as the law will allow. Extremely high (and in my judgment, unrealistic) expectations of marriage still are held. Disillusionment is bound to follow in the wake of such idealized romantic love. People just are not prepared for morning bad breath, business fatigue, premenstrual tensions, in-laws, and money running out before the month does. As one comedian said, "Marriage is like a steaming bath. Once you get used to it, it's not so hot."

* Andre Maurois, *Art of Living*. New York: Harper and Row, 1940, p. 50.

While most marriages remain monogamous, we are seeing more multiple marriages—"installment plan polygamy."

Some like Margaret Mead advocate a "two-stage" marriage in which there would be no legalized commitment by a man and a woman to each other until they had tested the relationship and until they were ready to have children. Many college-age couples follow this pattern now.

Still others challenge altogether the words of the marriage service that "God has established marriage for the welfare and happiness of mankind." In their search for utopia, they turn to communal living experiments to discover what most people try to find within the family. In our day, the best-known is the Israeli kibbutz. In the nineteenth century, a great many communes were created, many with deep religious motivations, as the avenue to intimacy, to a sense of belonging. Group ownership, group marriage, free love or celibacy substituted for the exclusive arrangements of the usual marriage. Hundreds of such groups have now formed in the Western countries, many of them calling themselves "the family." We are just beginning to understand the strengths and weaknesses of communes in fulfilling the goals traditionally satisfied by marriage. It is apparent that strong group discipline is necessary in successful communes; the anarchist could not function in such an arrangement.

In our day we will see much experimentation in men-women relationships. But before throwing out the traditional marriage, young people might well begin to do what the social scientists have been doing for some time: distinguishing between *types* of marriage relationships and discovering what it is that creates one type and not another. For example, Drs. John F. Cuber and Peggy Harroff, in their book, *The Significant Americans*, describe five distinct kinds of marriage relationships: the conflict-habituated, the devitalized, the passive-congenial, the vital, and the total. In one of the vital marriages, a husband says:

"I cheerfully, and that's putting it mildly, passed up two good promotions because one of them would have required some traveling and the other would have taken evening and week-end time—and that's when Pat and I *live*. The hours with her (after twenty-two years of marriage) are what I live for. You should meet her . . ." *

We need to find out what makes marriages like that possible. Can such a marriage come about when two people are pressured into marriage by parents or pregnancy, when they marry a parent symbol, when they marry simply because they need to be needed, or because they are lonely or insecure? This is a marriage which is a good example of creative fidelity, and it is possible if two people are happily married to themselves before they are married to each other.

Love needs caring. Rollo May says that care is a state in which something *matters* to a person. The opposite of apathy and indifference, caring is active concern for the other's life. It is not doing for him what he can do for himself, for that would make him childishly dependent, but it is being delighted that one can meet at least partially the needs of a loved one. This means sensing how to increase the other's satisfaction and security. This applies not only to personal relationships, but it also is in reference to the dispossessed and the alienated. This is what *agapé* means.

In the now famous folk-rock musical, "Hair," the pro-sex, pro-drugs, anti-Establishment "tribe" (commune) loudly proclaims love as its credo, embraces astrology and other mystical arts for inspiration, and turns on with group sex and chemical comforters. What is lacking is real *caring*. Jeanie, the pregnant acid head, wanders around like a lost soul; no one really befriends her. Sheila loves Berger but she is exhorted by the

* Dr. John F. Cuber and Dr. Peggy Harroff, *The Significant Americans: A Study of Sexual Behavior Among the Affluent.* New York: Appleton–Century, Affiliate of Meredith Press, p. 56.

tribe not to have a "hangup" about him, but to let anyone "love" her. Claude is drafted after much struggle, and when he returns, shorn of hair and in uniform, the tribe *cannot see him.* They turn him into a non-person. With all the "sheer fun" that is claimed for the play, it turns out to be a very sad commentary on the desperate search for meaning and love in our days. What is missing is what someone has called the essence of the life of Jesus—caring.

5.

Impatience and

Aggression

"Death is in the air," a radio commentator said recently in describing the atmosphere of our time. Young people may sense this more deeply than others because they are the first generation who never have known a time when nuclear war did not threaten total annihilation. Add to that the specter of asphyxiating gases, napalm, and bacterial agents, and you begin to see the extent of our orientation toward death. Other forms of destruction frighten us, too, some of them more than war: violent student rebellions, black militant and police riots, skyjacking and destruction of airplanes, bombing and arson in the cities. To many it appears that the orderly world is coming apart at the seams.

Much of the destruction and violence is the product of impatience and the inability to wait and to work for change. We see little evidence of "frustration tolerance," one of the key qualities of maturity in a nation or an individual. It is puzzling to know what turns many affluent young people into terrorists. I am convinced it is not only a revolutionary ideology but that it is also a lack of inward discipline and ability to channel anger into constructive change. One perceptive columnist wrote as follows about the SDS Weathermen killed in an improvised "bomb factory" in New York City:

"If you look at the short busy biographies of some of these people, you'll see they rarely stick to any one project long.

For six months they'll try community organization, then it's back to campus agitation, then building radical caucuses in labor unions, then high school organizing, then something else . . . Three years . . . five or six political projects. But the studied patience of long term work is generally foreign to them . . . The rich, white revolutionary terrorist has, through arrogance, absolutism, and recklessness . . . isolated himself until he has run out of choices; he can give up politics or become a clandestine bomb-thrower." *

Even Karl Marx stressed the unromantic, disciplined, long-range work of organizing people and educating for revolution. He knew how to play a waiting game.

Others of this generation want a chance to live. They want no more talk of killing, of military adventures, of home-made bombs and nuclear missiles. They are asking whether the destructive behavior of people can be curbed. They wonder if Christianity's promise that you can be "transformed by the renewal of your mind" is a pipe dream. They are eager to know if William James' "moral equivalent of war" is really feasible. Such young people oppose not only the revolutionary terrorist, but a large part of the American public, as well. A large proportion of the population is not averse to violence, either officially sanctioned or unregulated. They agree with the point of view attributed to United States Army General George S. Patton. At the opening of the tremendously popular film, "Patton," he declares that, traditionally, Americans love to fight, that all talk about them not wanting to fight is nonsense; further, that "all real Americans" love battle, they love a winner, and they will not tolerate losing. Because Americans hate the thought of losing, America will never lose a war, Patton says.

This impressive, pistol-packing, "religious," violent, yet kind-hearted man was speaking for countless people.

Young people today who are struggling to eliminate or re-

* Nicholas Von Hoffman, from *Why the Rich Toss Bombs, Washington Post*, March 20, 1970.

channel violence have the odds against them. Not only the terrorists but also respected public figures and law enforcement agencies demonstrate a lack of discipline and self-control. While condemning the students who goaded the National Guardsmen at Kent State University, the President's Commission on Campus Unrest said that the "indiscriminate" gunfire that killed four students and wounded nine others was "unnecessary, unwarranted, and inexcusable." Further, the commission found that the tragic deaths at Jackson State, where two students were killed, was due to an "over-reaction" by the Mississippi Highway Patrol and city police, acting partially out of racial animosity.

WHAT IS THE SOURCE?

First, let us get straight what we mean by "destructive aggression." The word "aggression" by itself is not adequate because it sometimes simply means "active," as in, "He is an aggressive salesman." "Anger" or "hostility" are not sufficient, either, because they refer to an emotional state, and not necessarily to behavior. One can kill or harm others without even being angry at them. "Violence" comes closest to describing the behavior we are talking about, although this, too, falls short—a parent, for instance, takes violent action to snatch a child from the path of a car. I use the phrase, "destructive aggression," to mean the actual *behavior, the goal of which is to inflict injury or destruction on persons, or to prevent their growth and development*. It is apparent that one can be destructively aggressive with words as well as with weapons.

Why are we destructively aggressive? What is the source of our violence? The behavioral sciences cannot explain all violence or its causes. There are three main theories concerning the origins of man's violence toward others. One is that man is instinctively disposed to violence. This tends to be the theory of Sigmund Freud and those who follow him, such as Konrad Lorenz and Robert Ardrey. Destructive aggression is seen as a boiler-like force which *somehow* must be expressed. According to this theory, the best that man can do is to find acceptable targets, or scapegoats, and to drain off aggressive drives by acting against a common enemy or danger.

A second theory sees destructive aggression arising out of frustration of human drives, goals, or desires. Aggression is not the only way to react to frustration, but it is a common response. When a person is thwarted in achieving his desires, he often wants to injure or destroy anyone or anything he feels is in the way. Thus, when the blacks who have become aware (through TV, among other things) of the standard of life they might have, are thwarted by legal and social barriers in attaining their aspirations, they may react with violence.

Middle-class whites, feeling their property, their way of life, and their security threatened by radicals of the New Left, may support a "backlash" of violence in order to control or repress anything seen as a "revolutionary" movement. Destructive aggression is not the *only* response to frustration. Some people react, instead, with apathy; others try to overcome the obstacles; still others change their goals or aspirations. There is also the aggressive, disciplined, non-violent reaction that is reminiscent of Gandhi and other spiritual leaders. If we take this "frustration-aggression" theory seriously, and I think we must, we then can think of how to create conditions that will reduce the frustrations of human beings and their violence.

A third theory holds that destructive aggression is learned, largely through imitating others who are engaging in violence or who are being rewarded for violent behavior. Thus when a parent spanks a child, he may think punishment will put a stop to the child's behavior. However, the child also learns from his parents an aggressiveness that he might use on his sister or his dog a few minutes later. Current research is revealing that the violence on TV and in the movies tends to make most people more ready to do violence. When we consider that, by the time he is 18, the average child has watched 20,000 hours of TV, during which about 13,000 human beings have been violently destroyed, we no longer are puzzled by the "emotional blunting," by the ease with which violence is accepted by the children and adults alike.

Each theory seems useful in understanding why man is so violent. The first—the theory of an innately aggressive drive —is not as well-accepted as the others at present. We like to think we can do something about man's violence, and the second and third theories assert that we *can* change things. We'd like to believe that man is not blindly destined to act out an instinct of destruction.

There are two mental mechanisms which are seen so often in connection with violence that they are considered almost universal: "projection" and "displacement." *Projection* is the tendency to see in others the characteristics we dislike in ourselves—characteristics we often refuse to recognize or simply disown.

Disowned anger toward others is seen as *their* anger toward us. In the absence of facts, projection reigns. A white woman may be attracted to a black man, but be unable to admit this to herself. She projects her feelings and so imagines that the desire exists in *him*, that he, and perhaps all other black men have sexually aggressive feelings towards her. This is why Jesus spoke of removing the log from your own eye before you attempt to remove the speck from the eye of another.

Displacement is the mental act of acquiring a substitute object for feelings of hostility because it is too dangerous to express these feelings to the real target. The captain scolds the first mate, the first mate the seaman, the seaman kicks his cat, etc. The target is usually an "out group" and vulnerable in cases of prejudice, because it is a group that cannot easily strike back. A person who is deeply frustrated by life and by his own goals might pick another target for his aggression. One commentator, noting the hostility between the "hard hats" and the liberal groups on campus, has said:

". . . Unlike the blacks today and unlike whites during the Depression, they are not excluded from the American pie;

they are part of the American dream. Only what kind of dream is it to return from spirit-mangling work to payments on the car, a mortgage on the house, stultifying TV programs, an over-heated teen-age daughter and a D-in-English, car-smashing son? But who, particularly in the Church, has had the candor and courage to tell them of their wrong dreams, to tell them that the wonders of man do not consist in consumer goods, to tell them that their wretchedness is interior and therefore it is wrong to scapegoat long-haired students and liberal professors . . ." *

VALUES ON A COLLISION COURSE

We are witnessing in our time a clash of values, a clash of cultures within Western culture, which are bound to create conflict. Much of that conflict is violent and destructive, and more can be expected. If the needs of one group are satisfied, the needs of another group are frustrated—or so it seems.

For example, there is the perpetual battle between the "haves" and the "have nots." One of the new values of youth is equality; because the good things of life are available in abundance, everyone should share them, rich and poor, black and white, male and female, underdeveloped and overdeveloped countries. There is little reason to expect, from the evidence of history that the rich can be persuaded to give up voluntarily the privileges they regard as their birthright, or as the product of their hard work and self-sacrifice. Those who hold four aces in their hand will not ask for a new deal. This is why revolution by peaceful means seems to be an historical rarity. Most often the powerful members of any society attempt to defend their privileges through military control of a country. If democratic methods fail to improve the lot of the "have nots," any culture is in deep trouble. President John F. Kennedy put the issue succinctly: "Those who make peaceful revolution impossible, make violent revolution inevitable."

* The Rev. William Sloan Coffin in *Motive*, January, 1970, p. 35.

Most young people are not revolutionaries in the sense that they feel the Establishment must be demolished, and that a new system of economics should be adopted in the United States. Dr. Jeffery Hadden, who studied 2,000 college seniors, found that fully 61 per cent agreed with this statement: "The free-enterprise system is the single economic system compatible with the requirements of personal freedom and constitutional government."

In 1969, CBS commissioned a study of college and non-college young people to determine the climate of youth opinion. They found that only 1 per cent could be classified as "violent revolutionaries," those who would destroy the system, if need be, by force and assault upon authorities. (It should be noted, however, that 1 per cent of those between 18 and 25 years of age is approximately 100,000 people). Ten per cent of the young people polled were classified as "radical dissidents," who felt that force and coercion were justified to make changes, but to a lesser degree; 23 per cent were called "reformers," and 48 per cent "moderates," both groups seeing the institutions of the country (business, the courts, the military, schools, political parties) as riddled with injustice, racism, and unnecessary violence. The reformers were more inclined than the moderates to try to do something about this. Only 19 per cent of the young people (many more non-college than college) were "conservatives," feeling that the American way of life was superior to all others. They emphasized property rights, work as the way to social mobility, and the necessity of obedience to existing authority. Fully 94 per cent of the whole sample, however, believed that society needed *some* legally based authority to prevent chaos and anarchy.

Among a minority of young people, it is clear, a new culture is forming that rejects many values of former generations. This minority is in conflict with the dominant culture. The movements within that minority react to this conflict in different ways. For example, the hippie subculture attempts to drop out of society and form its own microcosm as a foreign body within it. This group is in striking contrast to revolutionary activism which attempts by any means to overthrow the entire society and set up an alternative to it. The hippie protest is relatively peaceful. It represents the refusal of predominantly upper-middle class young people to continue their parents' pattern of life. They regard it as an empty way of life. They renounce modern industrial society in favor of a pastoral kind of existence, a search for utopia and for pleasing internal feelings and, often, for communion with nature. The hippie culture is an assault on most of the middle-aged values of affluent America: its commercialism, its new-car culture, its sexual restraint, its fear of stimulation. Psychedelic colors, erotic books and films, amplified sound all offend moderate, middle-class senses. The revolt against clothes "in good taste," against hygiene and against work as the god of life, all clash with the values of Western culture.

Many of these young people use drugs in an attempt to escape the world or culture in which they have been raised. Drugs (and adults can misuse them, too) tend to blunt anxiety, to offer a way to avoid awareness of the discontent necessary to change self and society. The basic mood is rejection and escape from the mainstream of society. Hippies want "salvation now." Militant revolutionaries condemn them for not trying to change the world, but most hippies view the militants' destructive aggression with great suspicion, feeling that through it they would become as immoral as the "oppressors" they were fighting.

Needless to say, many of my generation regard the hippies as a dangerous "counter culture" and subversive and immoral, as well. This group could well become society's new scapegoat, in place of blacks, since hippies are easily recognized by their appearance. In many towns, people with long hair, are looked upon with suspicion *regardless of their behavior*. We should remember that man looks upon the outward appearances and God looks within the heart. We need not agree with the hippies' style of life, but it is important that Christians not judge others by outward signs alone. We must try to understand the terrible conflict of values that leads young people to drop out of society, to reject its prized institutions so completely.

For example, how has the church let them down in their search for God, their search for something and someone to be true to, their quest for a way to change the values of society, to escape what they see as a meaningless rat-race for so many adults? If Jesus were to walk among the hippies and to talk with them, an excited response would not surprise me. In him they would recognize the love and purpose for which many of them have been looking. They could meet him face-to-face, not through a smoky haze of marijuana or incense.

Some young people have been drawn into a *militant revolutionary movement*. Their outrage at the Establishment seems to elicit the idealistic support of many youth. At the moment, the hostility of the radical left is directed toward the Indochina war and racism at home. These young people are enraged by the prospect of being drafted into a war which they feel nobody really wanted, to fight for goals nobody can spell out, in an area where few believe a war can be won. But deeper still is their animosity toward the technocracy of a society, capitalistic *or* communistic, which is run by experts, depends on science for its knowledge, and tends to shape man into a machine (see Theodore Roszak's *The Making of a Counter Culture*).

There is a revulsion against economic abundance for the few, against production for production's sake, and against making money, in general. Until recently, the New Left's methods have been to shock and offend and, increasingly, to destroy property, especially when it is owned by some faceless corporation, such as a large bank. (Incidentally, the aggressive confrontations of this group are not uncontrolled anger, but are deliberately planned, and are based on a knowledge of human reactions. For example, extremist leaders will find a neatly dressed coed who is willing to stand up and rattle off her propagandistic speech, laced with obscenities. This is designed to "blow the mind" of any middle-aged parent, who naturally thinks of his own daughter when he sees the speaker. The effect often is shock and confusion, if not anger, and this makes it impossible for him to think rationally and act coolly.)

We cannot predict how far the militant revolutionary will go in carrying out the work of destruction. They have given up on non-violent appeals for change: the courts, the sit-ins, the freedom marches, the political process, the poverty program. The violent tacticians of the New Left must have "victory" by next Wednesday or burn down the institution. Such impatience is beginning to lead to the use of guns, firebombs, even kidnapping in their own kind of tyranny which is born of their need for instant control, for expression of hatred. Restraint may be a tactical necessity but it is increasingly rare.

THE FRUITS OF AGGRESSION

I am convinced that the fruits of destructive aggression are evil. A modern society built on violence usually becomes more cruel, more dictatorial. Obviously, some things do change when a leader is assassinated. But what is the long-term result? Does not the successor fear the same thing will happen to him and so he becomes more totalitarian? Revolutions today tend to become dictatorships frankly dependent upon military or police power.

Destructive violence begets violence in reaction to it. This is why Jesus said, "All who take the sword will perish by the sword" (Matthew 26:52). This is what the American Civil Liberties Union meant when it warned the militants that their violence is self-defeating and counter-productive. It is leading everywhere to a backlash—in legislatures, among college administrators, among the police, among the majority of the people. It decreases freedom for all, because it increases the need for control.

Destructive aggression on a broad scale polarizes the people. Humane goals cannot be achieved through it. As soon as open hostility and violence begin, moderate ideas become the first casualties. Extremists from both sides, left and right, force people to take one side and be defined as an enemy by the other side. It is, of course, to the advantage of the extremist to push things into neat "good-evil" divisions. Add to their cause a few "martyrs" who have died in a "confrontation," and the battle is on. Suicidal conflict can be averted only if the clear-thinking, critical, man in the middle position remains strong.

Those who engage in destructive aggression often speak of it as a "tactic," as if it could be turned on and off like water. But violence is addictive and contagious. It is addictive in that it gives one a temporary, heady feeling of power and, therefore, is easier to use next time. It is contagious in that violence spreads violence. A mass killing by a deranged student in Texas set off other people on killing sprees elsewhere. The contagion of violence is seen in time of war. So-called legiti-mate violence, on behalf of one's country, provokes much "illegimate" violence in every sphere of life. Many people are drawn to violence like moths to a flame. So-called "good vio-lence"—violence in the service of a good cause—can easily become violence in the service of a bad cause. Destructive aggression spreads like a forest fire. It cannot be turned on and off.

WE MAKE LEGITIMATE THE EVIL WE DO

None of us can afford to be self-righteous and point the finger at the "violent ones." We all are potentially violent and destructive. Years ago the famous theologian, Reinhold Niebuhr, wrote a book entitled *Moral Man and Immoral So-ciety*. Its theme was that we do evil as members of a group or of a society that we never would do as individuals with a conscience. Under what circumstances can we engage in *guilt-free* violence? What circumstances promote a "moral anes-thesia" within us?

Authority has a powerful effect for good or evil on people in any society. We all know about the trial of Adolph Eichmann who, when he was accused of killing thousands of Jews in Nazi

Germany, answered, "I was given my orders." Even a heinous crime can be excused on the basis of responsibility to duty, or loyalty to one's leaders. But, you may ask, wouldn't people raised in a democratic nation be less likely to follow authority blindly? Our best evidence suggests that this is not the case. The now-famous Milgram study, carried on at Yale University, demonstrated to what extent well-educated people living in a democracy were inclined to blindly obey an authority. A man posing as a scientific authority ordered them to give what they thought were electric shocks (actually, the machine was rigged so that no shocks were administered) to a man in another room each time he made a mistake in calculation. The shocks supposedly were increased in intensity with each mistake made. Even though they had evidence that the other person was suffering and in pain, 60 per cent of the subjects continued to administer the "shocks" until the very end of the series. When you can make "the authority" accountable for what you do to someone else, it may be quite easy for many people to engage in destructive actions without feeling guilty. What does the authority do to make it easy for us to engage in guilt-free aggression?

First, the authority *labels the appropriate targets of aggression*. These are the enemy, the out-group. Depending upon the particular authority we honor, they will be called various names: traitor, pig, militant, racist, liberal, subversive, Jew, Viet Cong, etc. They are seen as dangerous to us and are labeled bad, sick, or crazy. Because we must protect ourselves from them, we extoll the rightness of our cause. We now have *moral* justification for destructive aggression against them—and no guilt.

Second, we always need to see ourselves as engaging in *reactive aggression*; that is, responding to an enemy's own aggression. "He started it" was our retort as children when scolded for fighting. Every group that engages in violence sees its enemy as the one who started it; even Hitler did this. Each side of a conflict sees the other side as deliberate, as malicious, and as powerful. Someone else did it first.

Third, to make destructive aggression legitimate, we must *perceive the enemy as less than human*. He does not have feelings or fears or a family, as we have. He doesn't hope, or love, or hate, or suffer. He is not human; he is a "gook," a "Jap," a "nigger," a "honky," a "savage." For this to work, however, a society must keep its people from knowing those in the out-groups as people. As much as possible, it must prevent contact between them. Otherwise we might discover that "they" are human, too.

Fourth, the more *anonymous* we can become, the less guilty we are about our aggression. We act in large groups or mobs or armies. We disguise ourselves in white sheets or uniforms. Where all are guilty and not identifiable, no one is guilty.

Seeing how we legitimate the evil we do, what does it mean for a Christian to be "*in* this world but not *of* this world?" What does it mean to "render unto Caesar that which is Caesar's and to God that which is God's"? Nothing in Jesus' teaching would suggest that the state or government be elevated to a position of *supreme* loyalty in the life of the Christian. After being challenged by the High Priest, an agent of the government of Rome, Peter replied, "We must obey God rather than man" (Acts 5:29, New English Bible). In ancient Israel, the prophet Elijah, at great personal risk, confronted the ruler Ahab. And when Ahab called him "a disturber of Israel" (doesn't that have a contemporary sound?), Elijah replied that it was Ahab who was a disturber of Israel's peace, for his rule rejected God's commandments to be humane.

We must not underestimate the tremendous conflict of loyalties in a Christian's life, the problems of how to follow the teachings of Jesus in a secular society, especially when a government demands loyalty to itself, instead of being "under God."

BLESSED ARE THE PEACEMAKERS

St. Francis' well-known prayer begins, "Lord, make me an instrument of thy peace." Peace is deep. It involves the self, the enemy, the society in which one lives. We must do more than put band-aids on the world's hemorrhaging heart. Christian peacemakers need to explore disciplined, non-violent resistance to the evils of society. The late Dr. Leslie Cooke pointed up the necessity for the church to throw its full weight behind every legitimate demand for social, economic, and racial justice. He said:

". . . the trouble with the Christian church is this: that it is frightened to recognize and acknowledge the revolution which it started. And it is becoming a violent revolution because we abandoned it when we ought to have been making nonviolent revolution." *

Young people unacquainted with the teachings of the Old Testament prophets and of Jesus may not realize just how revolutionary the Judaic-Christian tradition is, how it really calls for turning upside down the values of the church and of society. Two samples:

"Hear the word of the Lord, you rulers of Sodom;
　attend, you people of Gomorrah, to the instruction of
　　　　　our God:
　　Your countless sacrifices, what are they to me?
　　　　says the Lord
　　I am sated with whole-offering of rams
　　　　and the fat of buffaloes;
　　I have no desire for the blood of bulls,
　　　　of sheep and of he-goats.
　. . . The reek of sacrifice is abhorrent to me.
　New moons and sabbaths and assemblies,
　sacred seasons and ceremonies, I cannot endure.
　. . . When you lift your hands outspread in prayer,
　I will hide my eyes from you.
　Though you offer countless prayers,
　　　　I will not listen.
　There is blood on your hands;

* Quoted by Robert S. Paul in *Presbyterian Life*, January 1, 1970, p. 31. Copyright 1970 by *Presbyterian Life*. Used by permission.

wash yourselves and be clean.
Put away the evil of your deeds,
    away out of my sight.
Cease to do evil and learn to do right,
pursue justice and champion the oppressed;
give the orphan his rights, plead the widow's cause.
. . . Your very rulers are rebels, confederate with
    thieves;
every man among them loves a bribe
    and itches for a gift;
    they do not give the orphan his rights,
and the widow's cause never comes before them"
           (Isaiah 1:10–17, 23 New English Bible).

* * *

"Then the king will say to those on his right hand, 'You have my father's blessing; come, enter and possess the kingdom that has been ready for you since the world was made. For when I was hungry, you gave me food; when thirsty, you gave me drink; when I was a stranger, you took me into your home, when naked you clothed me; when I was ill you came to my help, when in prison you visited me.' Then the righteous will reply, 'Lord, when was it we saw you hungry and fed you, or thirsty and gave you drink, a stranger and took you home, nor naked and clothed you? When did we see you in prison and come to visit you?' And the king will answer, 'I tell you this: anything you did for one of my brothers here, however humble, you did for me'" (Matthew 25:34–40 New English Bible).

This world is a tough place to change into that vision of the kingdom. This means that those who are instruments of peace must be toughened, disciplined, persistent, patient. Let me suggest a few of the qualities of the non-violent peacemaker:

A non-violent peacemaker has a *new concept of manhood*, patterned after the person of Jesus, gentle, firm, reconciling, and healing. Such a man does not conceal mistakes and errors in judgment, nor does he make false pride more important than compassion. His is the kind of courage which insists that loyalty to the truth is good for *all*, not merely for his tribe, family, or nation. A New Testament kind of man would accept responsibility for his own behavior, no matter what the circumstance. He ultimately is responsible only to the God he sees in Jesus. Such a man must combine openness with firmness, toughness with tenderness, conviction with self-criticism.

A non-violent peacemaker must *be at peace with himself*. He can neither fool himself nor despise himself. He will admit his feelings. When he feels competitive and hostile, he will not be horrified that he is capable of such emotions. He will learn to express his anger. The letter to the Ephesians states it clearly: "Be angry, but do not sin; do not let the sun go down on your anger, and give no opportunity to the devil." Actually, it is easier for most Christians to feel guilty than resentful, and it takes more courage for them to express anger than guilt. When you express guilt, you expect to pacify your opponent. Anger might stir up hostility in him.*

Further, a peacemaker must come to terms with his own fear. Much of the violence in the world comes from the fear of being hurt. Demogogic politicians always are reminding their people of the dangers of potentially hostile nations; they cultivate fear. Until we come to grips with our *own* fear and anxiety, we will not be able to help a society so driven by fear that it pursues policies which must lead to the very disasters it fears. As victims of fear, we seek security at the expense of others. Until I can ask, "What is the worst possible thing that could happen to me in this situation?", and am able to bear the answer, I am not living through my fear. Knowing that life is in God's hands, we can accept our fear, take our courage in both hands and act. "Fear not, for I am with you to the end of the age," were the words that transformed a collection

---

* See my *Christians in Families*, Chapter 8, for clues as to how to express anger.

of timid, ordinary people into a group with courage and a sense of adventure—the first Christian church.

If non-violence is "a determination not to violate the integrity of any human being . . .", we must eliminate destructive aggression toward *ourselves*. We can be violent in hating ourselves for not achieving our ideals or a state of perfection. This self-disgust spills over into constant criticism of others and anger toward them. The late Paul Tillich reminds us, "He who is able to love himself is able to love others also; he who has learned to overcome self-contempt has overcome his contempt for others . . . Sometimes it happens that we receive the power to say 'Yes' to ourselves, that peace enters us and makes us whole, that self-hate and self-contempt disappear and that our self is reunited with itself. Then we say that grace has come upon us." * Peacemakers are grace-full.

A non-violent peacemaker *learns to see his "enemy" in a new way*. In the Sermon on the Mount, Jesus said, "You have learned that they were told, 'Love your neighbor and hate your enemy.' But what I tell you is this: Love your enemies and pray for your persecutors." (Matthew 5:43, 44, New English Bible). The enemy is anyone we can be persuaded has hurt us or might hurt us. He is in part a product of our unadmitted fears, a result of propaganda, or a projection screen on which our own unacknowledged desires are thrown. In my enemy I really may see myself. Jesus does not try to persuade us there is no enemy. Someone actually may want to hurt us. He asks us to see him as *more than enemy* as another man with the feelings, the hopes, the fears we all have. Once I see him as another human being, wanting to be understood, to be loved, to be competent, I have a new vision of him and, hopefully, a new way to relate to him. He wants to be himself, as I do. Of course he does much evil, as I do. He is full of greed and prejudice, as I am. Only such recognition will reduce my fear and

* Paul Tillich, *The Shaking of the Foundations.* New York: Scribner's, 1948, p. 158, 163.

hatred of him. If the enemy ceases to be an abstraction, perhaps human contact is possible. He is no longer a "pig" or "radical" or "racist" or "Establishment." He is me. Remembering that he wants what I want, perhaps we can find fulfillment together.

The non-violent peacemaker *disciplines himself to learn how to resist evil without destroying persons.* Peacemaking does not mean accepting the evil in a society. Non-violence is not passive; it means active resistance. Until an adversary knows that non-violent men are willing to suffer for their beliefs, he will not really listen to them. Harvey Seifert, a profound student of non-violence, has written of persuasion, negotiation, political action and economic pressure as the basic non-violent methods to be used in seeking social change. These methods, he has indicated, will only infrequently be pushed to such unconventional lengths that suffering will be the result; yet, at all times, these four methods should be accompanied by willingness to suffer.

In his book, *Conquest by Suffering,* Seifert observes that the non-violent peacemaker is *patient.*

> "Persistence plus patience is a strange formula for minds that deal in distorted blacks and whites. A thoughtless passion for sudden results often leads to self-defeating violence. It seems obvious to the Neanderthal men among us that the quickest way with opposition is to knock it into line with overwhelming power. . . . In foreign policy, impatient, trigger-happy zealots may want to call out the Marines to crash through every variety of impediment. This easily becomes a stone-ax approach in an environment of delicate electronic machinery." *

The non-violent peacemaker *must have a conviction that his efforts are in line with the basic direction of life.* No one has put this better than the late Dr. Martin Luther King:

* Harvey Seifert, *Conquest by Suffering.* Philadelphia: The Westminster Press, 1968, p. 183. Copyright © MCMLXV, W. L. Jenkins. Used by permission.

"Nonviolent resistance is based on the conviction that the universe is on the side of justice. Consequently, the believer in nonviolence has deep faith in the future. This faith is another reason why the nonviolent resister can accept suffering without retaliation. For he knows that in the struggle for justice, he has cosmic companionship. It is true that there are devout believers in nonviolence who find it difficult to believe in a personal God. But even those persons believe in the existence of some creative force that works for universal wholeness. Whether we call it an unconscious process, an impersonal Brahman, or a Personal Being of matchless power and infinite love, there is a creative force in this universe that works to bring the disconnected aspects of reality into a harmonious whole. . . . The cross is the eternal expression of the length to which God will go to restore broken commmunity." *

Man is not alone when he is an instrument of peace.

* Martin Luther King, *Stride Toward Freedom.* New York: Harper, 1958, pp. 105, 106, 107.

6.

Hope—in the Present Tense

The most painful experience of a person's life is meaninglessness. When life no longer makes sense, when the present seems dead, when the future seems impossible, and when the dearest relationships are shallow or broken, we are cursed with a sense of emptiness. None of us escapes that feeling of a terrible void sometime in life. The collapse of meaning has plagued every age and section of life. It has been expressed in many ways:

> "Life . . . is a tale
> Told by an idiot, full of sound and fury.
> Signifying nothing."
> (Macbeth, Act V, Scene 5)

***

"Life is a lie, my sweet. . . . It builds green trees that ease your eyes and draws you under them. Then when you're here in the shade and you breathe in and say, 'Oh God, how beautiful,' that's when the bird on the branch lets go his droppings and hits you on the head."
(Arthur L. Kopit, "Oh, Dad, Poor Dad, Mama's Hung You In the Closet and I'm Feeling So Sad." New York: Hill and Wang, 1960)

***

> "My God, my God, why hast thou forsaken me?"
> (Jesus of Nazareth—Psalm 22 and Matthew 27)

84

***

"Here is what frightens me. To lose one's life is a little thing, and I will have the courage when necessary. But to see the sense of life dissipated, to see our reason for existence disappear: that is what is unsupportable. A man cannot live without reason."

(Cherea, in Albert Camus' *Caligula and Three Other Plays.* New York: Alfred A. Knopf, Inc., p. 21)

***

"Good Lord, where are You?
  If you really do exist,
  Why don't you come out of hiding
  And do something about this creature in distress?
"I am physically weary;
  I am mentally depressed;
  I am spiritually defeated.
  I can't eat; I can't sleep.
  I am like garbage, discarded refuse in the back alley;
  Like yesterday's newspaper shuffled around by the
     wind.
  I feel like some sort of zombi,
  Some nonentity, some nothing that people, if they
     acknowledge, would only curse."

(Paraphrase on Psalm 102, from Leslie Brandt's, *Good Lord, Where are You?* St. Louis: Concordia Publishing House, 1967, p. 54.)

***

Linus: "Life is difficult, isn't it, Charlie Brown?"
Charlie Brown: "Yes it is."
Linus: "But I've developed a new philosophy. . . . I
     dread only one day at a time."

(From "Peanuts," *San Francisco Chronicle*, August 8, 1966)

Have you been through any of these experiences? Does Linus seem to have the last word? Well, there is another word—"hope." To many, hope seems no answer to meaninglessness.

Modern as well as ancient writers have seen hope as a whimpering escape from the hard realities of life. Camus, a case in point, says that *both* suicide and hope are retreats from the courage to accept the absurdity of life and to live courageously within it. Samuel Beckett, in *Waiting for Godet*, portrays hope as a resigned, passive, ineffectual waiting.

But somehow the word, "hope," persists in our daily vocabulary and appears regularly in the journals of poets, philosophers, psychiatrists, even urban sociologists. Perhaps we don't really understand hope; perhaps we confuse it with optimism.

WHY NOT OPTIMISM?

Americans have traditionally been an optimistic people. According to American mythology, the possibilities for any man are unlimited if he's willing to work. The skies are open; the frontiers beckon. We claim that the aspiration is the man; I am not what I have been or what I am now, but what I seek. Education sometimes is seen as offering every man the chance to become a king. Society may still be somewhat of a jungle in which we must struggle to survive and should struggle to succeed, but progress is inevitable. These views represent a naive optimism. An optimist has been defined as someone who believes this is the best of all possible worlds; a pessimist as someone who is afraid the optimist is right. But progress no longer is considered inevitable. With every step toward rationality, we seem to move more deeply into irrational behavior. Many of us have come to see the "shadow side" of progress; that by virtual genocide this nation wrested its soil from a people who were here earlier; that a portion of the nation's wealth was built upon enslavement of a black minority, still kept "in its place" 100 years after emancipation. Many of us have begun to doubt that America is truly, and without ulterior motives, a beneficent helper of the poor nations of the world.

Technological advances have given many an optimistic outlook. They hold great promise of improving the quality of life. Yet they have their dark underside, as well, and this does not mean only the weapons of a nuclear age. There is also the emerging possibility of biological and psychological transformations, already in the laboratory, that will deprive men of any real freedom and a meaningful future. This recital of faults is not merely "high I.Q. whimpering on a cosmic scale" that existentialists have been accused of by the optimists. The gap between the have and have-not nations of the world is *growing;* the gap between the have and have-not citizens of the United States is *widening,* in spite of our technological advances.

Technological advances don't always help. The rate of change in our way of living is so rapid that it has produced bewilderment, frustration, and disorientation. Alvin Toffler calls this reaction "future shock." The premature arrival of the future is apparently one factor which gives rise to mass irrationality, to a desperate clinging to the familiar, and to a marked increase in violence.

Other signs of "dis-ease" give the lie to the optimistic view. We note an increase in despair among many young people, especially in the large cities. I worked for awhile in San Francisco as a group counselor for young adults who had attempted suicide. The word "hopeless" was frequently on their lips. Translated, I discovered that most often they really meant "helplessness" and "loneliness." There was a tendency to see the future as bleak, as holding out for them neither competence nor love. This is what the psychotherapist, Ira Progoff, calls the "Never Syndrome," the feeling that one never will achieve his deepest desires.

American mythology also has held that if you can live in a suburb, in your own home, you will find constant happiness. We know now that life in the suburbs also can produce a profound boredom which Harvard sociologist David Reisman has called the "suburban sadness." There can be a pervasive sense of "stuckness"—stuckness with one's job, with one's spouse, with the low-keyed monotony which pervades gardening and cocktail parties alike. T. S. Eliot might have been speaking of Americans rather than commuting Londoners when he wrote:

"A Cry from the North, from the West and from the South
Whence thousands travel daily to the timekept City;
Where My Word is unspoken,
In the land of lobelies and tennis flannels,
The rabbit shall burrow and the thorn revisit,
The nettle shall flourish on the gravel court,
And the wind shall say, 'Here were godless people:
Their only monument the asphalt road
And a thousand lost golf balls.' " *

BETWEEN OPTIMISM AND DESPAIR

If one were left with only this negative picture of life, he might be overcome by pessimism, if not nihilism. If he denies the reality of such a picture, on the other hand, or believes that the remedy for such ills is simple, he is deceived by optimism. We need neither optimism nor pessimism. We need realistic hope, which lies between despair, on the one hand, and optimism on the other.

Hope can be born only when insecurity or evil are felt so profoundly that despair is the response. When it deserves its name, hope is *the way of overcoming despair.*

We try to deny our despair, our anxiety, and our insecurity in many ways. We keep everlastingly busy so we won't have to think about it. Or we look only at the positive in life and religion, forgetting there is a cross at the heart of Christian faith. But unless we pass *through* the valley of meaninglessness, hope cannot be born. Clinging to false security and a predictable life is not the way to genuine hope.

I think this is the meaning of the interview Jesus had with the rich young man, as recorded in Luke 18. The young man obviously was self-assured and secure, yet he was looking for more to life than he had. He had done everything expected of him; he had obeyed the Law and his parents since childhood;

* T. S. Eliot, Choruses from "The Rock," *Collected Poems* 1909–1962. New York: Harcourt Brace Jovanovich, Inc., 1963.

he had conformed to the standards of his community and had fulfilled the expectations of the best class of society. And God, apparently, had given him great wealth. Jesus, cutting to the heart of the matter, punctured this almost perfect picture by saying, "One thing you still lack!" Read Jesus' instructions to the rich young man to sell everything he had and give it to the poor. Get behind these words. What was Jesus after? The young man lacked a sense of *insecurity!* That's what he needed to move beyond the easy conformities, to risk his life for his fellow man and for God. If he could not see how insecure he really was, in spite of his "securities," how did he think he would find eternal life? Nothing damages real hope more than hiding from insecurity, death, and evil.

Now we can appreciate anew St. Paul's insistence that everyone lives by hope. Hope is the sense of possibility; in despair and trouble, it is the sense of a way out and a destiny that goes somewhere, even if not to the address one has in mind.

What Hope Is and What It Is Not

Hoping is imagining a future in which our potential might be fulfilled. Hoping carries the confidence that deep changes can occur in ourselves, and that we will be able to live life fully and effectively and usefully. Genuine hoping is not a bland sameness of mood; it alternates with despair and doubt.

Christian hope, as we began to see in Chapter II, does not stand or fall with specific "hopes," with concrete desires. When the psalmist declared, "My hope is in the Lord . . ." (Psalm 130) and St. Paul said, "Christ in you, the hope of a glory to come . . ." (Colossians 1:27, New English Bible), they were not telling life where it had to come out. Hope cannot predict that something *will* happen or that it *must* happen. Hope is convinced, rather, that the power of life which it taps will work out fulfillment according to the potential of a person at his time in history. St. Paul said, "In hope we are saved. Now hope which is seen is not hope. For who hopes for what he sees?" No, if the goal is clear, we must desire it enough to work for it. Hope is deeper than desire, it is the certainty that fulfillment is possible and, indeed, that fulfillment *is taking place*, even though we may not be aware of what is happening within us to make this possible.

Hope should not be confused with utopian fantasy or vague longings. Much of what is called hope really is desire wrapped up in illusions, as when we say wistfully, "I hope so much that . . ." Further, magic hope, in contrast to Christian hope, is wishing for something that will come easily without having to do anything about it, without any attention, or effort, or suffering. It is wishing, unrealistically, with hopes that are too high and, inevitably, disappointing. Because magic hope reaches for the impossible, it increases hopelessness. It lives almost entirely in the future instead of the present. Magic hope alternates between passive waiting, on the one hand, and forcing events before their time (*kairos*), on the other.

Christian hope is tied in with the biblical concept of the kingdom of God. It always offers *some* hope here and now, and a beginning is apparent if one has eyes to see. The kingdom of God is here now (like the mustard seed), but not yet here (as the fully developed tree). Without such a beginning, hope is misnamed. Hope starts with a person's potentialities; it does not outrun them, wildly imagining what cannot be. Unlike optimism, hope is aware of the many obstacles to its fulfillment, but in the face of them, we should neither fight the obstacles nor drift with them. We should yield as a swimmer yields to the sea.

We have spoken of usefulness giving significance to work. St. Francis expressed that in his famous prayer:

> "Lord, make me an instrument of Thy peace.
> Where there is hatred, let me sow love; where there
> is injury, pardon; where there is doubt, faith; *where
> there is despair*, hope; where there is sadness, joy;
> where there is darkness, light. . . ."

How do we sow hope where there is despair?

How Hope Is Renewed

The renewal of hope, in my experience, comes through four phases, although I am not sure everyone goes through all four phases.

The birth of hope often requires, *first, an interior journey.* In a time of discouragement, we often are advised to "get out and do something" or "forget yourself and get out with other people." Sometimes this helps, but often it distracts us only temporarily from our emptiness. Darkness usually returns when we stop running. This is why so many of us get depressed when confined to bed with some ailment like the flu. We can no longer run and we are face-to-face with ourselves.

There is a pilgrimmage through this despair that may lead to hope, and it is based on the assumption that change occurs when we experience fully the pain we are in now, *not* when we are trying to be something we are not.

If we can enter suffering fully, and also talk about our feelings, a change will take place. This is a paradox recognized both by Christian experience throughout the centuries and by modern psychology.* Forget what you should be or should feel, and recognize what you honestly feel in your soul. Learn how to:

> "Throw away the lights, the definitions,
> And say of what you see in the dark
> That it is this or that it is that,
> But do not use rotted names. . . .
> Nothing must stand
> Between you and the shapes you take
> When the crust of shape has been destroyed." †

The "rotted names" are labels we put on ourselves to say we are "not O.K."; they express how we judge and scold ourselves

* See *The Choice is Always Ours,* edited by Dorothy Phillips. New York: Harper & Row, 1960.
† From "The Man with the Blue Guitar," *The Collected Poems of Wallace Stevens.* New York: Alfred A. Knopf, 1954, p. 183.

for our feelings. Walking through the valley of the shadow of death, we feel opposite feelings and images emerge—not only despair, but hope; love as well as hate; tranquillity as well as anxiety; even, perhaps, an image of God—"I will fear no evil, for Thou art with me." An image of the future often emerges with this honest facing of one's experience.

In his book, *The Symbolic and the Real*, Ira Progoff gives a fascinating description of the transformation of negative experiences through creative patience. An acorn has the potentiality of an oak tree; a lion cub the potentiality for becoming a full-grown lion. Their growth unfolds naturally, unless there is serious interference. So, also, human beings have a seed of potentiality within them. Man, however, is not driven entirely by instinct, such as that of the bird that builds the kind of nest characteristic of its species, even though it never has done so before.

Man, having the gift of self-consciousness, is not driven but lured by visions, symbols, and images—all part of his psyche. His imagination, whether he is awake or asleep, produces images of the potentiality that is possible for him. They tell him what he already is, to a certain degree; they give him intimations of what he might be, and hints of his life's meaning. When his energies are blocked by negative feelings, he cannot grasp the possibilities stretching before him. But when he recognizes his pain, calls it by name, even describes it by writing it down, something begins to happen. Willingness to live with pain releases the growth process again. Since life always is in motion, it begins to move forward and to unfold, as a tulip emerges from its bulb. Such growth requires *waiting*. This does not mean doing nothing; it does mean a willingness to listen to the pain within. This often gives us a sense of being connected in a deep way with life and its abundance. If we are willing to trust, to *go with* our pain and the darkness in our psyche, the growth process within us reverses its direction and turns to the outside world with new resources for coping with life. Our effective action in the outside world then serves to renew hope still further.

The *second* way hope is renewed is through *a growing awareness of our ability to influence life around us.*

To discover that we are able to do something about our situation is a hope-liberating discovery. This kind of discovery takes place on other levels of life, too. In one of Wolfgang Köhler's classic studies of the 1920's, the chimpanzee, Sultan, was enclosed in an area separated by bars from a room in which a banana was placed. It was just out of his reach, and he used one of two hollow bamboo sticks in an attempt to reach it. After a while he gave up trying and settled down to playing with the sticks. Playfully, he fit one stick into the other. Suddenly he realized that he had a long stick that might reach the banana. Very excited, he ran over to the bars. The realization of his new ability altered the situation, and Köhler reported that the chimp changed from hopelessness to hopefulness, that he was released to try again to reach the banana.

When a way to do something effective is realized—from an infant tying a shoe, to a college student finishing a research project, to a group of people organizing politically to accomplish a goal—hope rises. However, if the aspirations are too far above the power to achieve them, discouragement is born. When we promise something that cannot be delivered, we may increase despair. A little hope is a dangerous thing. For example, we have learned, painfully, that there is a greater possibility of violence from those who have come some distance from poverty than from those who have never realized that liberation from poverty might be possible. Despair and anger mount when people sense what *could be* but begin to think that, because of human selfishness, it will not be. When we arouse man's expectations, we had better follow through, or the disillusionment will be all the more bitter.

The power to influence life in today's corporate world may come principally through political action. Politics in the art of building and preserving power to change social arrangements. Political authority defines the space in which men can live together, both in restraint and in the pursuit of goals. The young are learning the art of organizing for political action, but pessimism concerning its effectiveness still pervades the youth scene. Such pessimism, however, is not confined to young people. An exceptionally talented man, John Gardner, a former government official, has said in a news dispatch:

> "Our political and governmental processes have grown so unresponsive, so ill-designed for contemporary purposes, that they waste taxpayers' money, mangle good programs, and smother every good man that gets into the system."

A new movement, The Common Cause, is being forged to reshape government and party politics at every level. If it increases our ability to influence politics, it will be an avenue of hope.

Thirdly, hope is renewed with the *development of nourishing human relationships*.

Hope is considered an interior strength by many, something one possesses alone. You can wish, or long, or day-dream as an individual, but hope is basically a shared experience. It is renewed through relationships. Hope is born when someone really *hears* us. The noted psychotherapist, Carl Rogers, reports this personal experience:

> "Not long ago a friend called me long distance about a certain matter. We concluded the conversation and I hung up the phone. Then, and only then did his tone of voice really hit me. I said to myself, behind the subject matter we were discussing, there seemed to be a note of distress, discouragement or even despair, which had nothing to do with the matter at hand. I felt this so sharply I wrote him a letter saying something to this effect—'I may be all wrong in what I am going to say, and if so, you can toss this in the wastebasket but to me after I had hung up the phone it sounded as though you were in real distress. . . .' Then I attempted to share with him some of my own feelings about him and about his situation in ways that I hoped might be helpful.

I sent off the letter with some real qualms. . . . I quickly received a reply. He was extremely grateful that someone had heard him. . . . I have often noticed in therapy and in groups that the more deeply I hear the meanings of the person the more there is that happens. One thing I have come to look upon as almost universal is that when a person has been deeply heard, there is a moistness in his eyes . . . It's as though he were saying, 'Thank God, somebody heard me. Someone knows what it's like to be me.' In such moments I have had the fantasy of a prisoner in a dungeon, tapping out day after day a Morse code message, 'Does anybody hear me? Is anybody there . . . ?' And finally one day he hears some faint tappings which spell out 'Yes.' And he is released from loneliness and has become a human being again." *

Helping involves entering the world of the other with understanding.

In the *fourth* place, hope is renewed when a group of human beings *share a corporate image of their future and begin to live in terms of it*. As the author of Proverbs put it, "Where there is no vision, the people perish."

Can young people create a vision of a world that is worth working for, worth waiting for, worth being whole for? Young people today are more aware of what they don't want than of what they do. They don't want war. They know the horror of the Indochina conflict. They also know, as Kenneth Keniston points out, the tale of three cities made famous during World War II: Auschwitz, Hiroshima, and Nuremberg. *Auschwitz* showed how a nation could embark upon a systematized, well-organized, scientific plan to exterminate an entire people. *Hiroshima* demonstrated how "clean," easy, and impersonal a cataclysm could be to those who perpetrate it, and how

* From an unpublished paper, "Some Elements of Effective Interpersonal Communication," by Carl Rogers.

demonic, shattering, and brutal it could be to those who experienced it. And *Nuremberg* underlined the principle that men have an accountability above obedience to national policy, a responsibility beyond loyalty to a nation's laws or to its officials. These are the lessons of history.

What positive images of the future are viable today? Writers by the score are creating imaginative paradises and technological utopias, ranging from Orwell's *1984* to Huxley's *Island*. Psychologists try their hand at it, as in *The Sane Society* (Erich Fromm) and *Walden Two* (B. F. Skinner). This is a day of utopia-building.

Through the centuries, Christians have petitioned: "Thy kingdom come, Thy will be done, on earth as it is in heaven." Church history records hundreds of attempts to detail that kingdom, to blueprint and schedule the future God has promised. Jesus warned that would get us nowhere; no one can read the mind of God nor control how he works. But people have persisted in their need for a vision of how it will all turn out. Vivid images of gates, golden streets, beasts, and lakes of fire are part of that effort. But what clues are there in Jesus' teachings about the kingdom?

When we look at what Jesus said concerning the kingdom (largely through his parables), we find that the kingdom is described almost wholly in pictures, in images drawn from the common experiences of men. The kingdom of God (or heaven) is like this—for example, a treasure hidden in a field. Or like that—for example, a great supper. Images crowd the mind as if the kingdom had so many qualities that exactly what it is like cannot be defined, beyond its being the reign of God in human affairs. One thing is clear: Jesus' idea of the kingdom was far deeper than the improvement of the outward conditions of life, although it included that. It always involves an inner transformation, as well as an outward change in human relationships. The kingdom of God is both *within* you and *among* you. And we have an intimation of what that kingdom will be like in Jesus' life, death, and resurrection.

A CHILD IN THE MIDST

One image of the kingdom to which young people and others might respond today concerns the importance of the child. Once when his disciples were anxious to get on with their journey, they stopped children from approaching Jesus. He told them, "Let the children come to me; do not hinder them for to such belongs the Kingdom of God" (Mark 10:14). Again, when he talked about what it means to welcome him into our lives, he said, "Whoever receives one such child . . . receives me" (Mark 9:37). When his disciples were debating as to who was the greatest in the kingdom, he put a child in the midst of them and said, "Unless you turn and become like children, you will never enter the Kingdom . . ." (Matthew 18:3) When he wanted to point up the most damning sins of human life, he said, "Whoever causes one of these little ones . . . to sin, it would be better for him to have a great millstone fastened around his neck and to be drowned in the depth of the sea." (Matthew 18:5). Obviously, he thought the child and childlikeness (not childishness) were crucial to the kingdom.

Let me suggest how this emphasis might contribute to the future that we would hope to create:

First of all, think about what a difference it would make if a child were to be the center of the world's values. If we were to reorder our lives according to what would be good for a child, would not many of our current policies and practices seem atrocious? No one who is not sick or alienated from life can hate or wish to destroy a baby, a newborn baby, the universal symbol of humanity. He is not yet an American, a Russian, a Japanese, a Vietnamese; he is a new bit of humanity, the incarnation of the universal concerns which could unite us. In the ashes of Pompeii, excavators found the skeleton of a deformed child with his mother's arm around him. Something universal is represented in that ancient scene. Surely the saddest picture of any war is an exhausted mother holding a child in the ruins of their home.

If a child were the center of our concerns, what would be the results of our treatment of poverty, racial injustice, education, health services—of war? Few stories have touched the world more deeply than the tragedy of Anne Frank. Few things could have dramatized the terror, the cruelty, the senselessness of the Nazi government as did that diary of her life. It stretches one's imagination—as Jesus always wanted to do—to visualize how those in power might change their policies if a child were central to their thinking concerning the social and economic conditions they help to arrange. Were that vision kept alive, people would not perish.

Jesus' words, "of such is the kingdom," also suggest that the recovery of childlike qualities will lead to meaning and vitality in life. Some older commentaries on Jesus' teaching state that obedience was the characteristic Jesus had in mind as he pointed to the child's nature. I think they are wrong. Jesus, rather, stressed freedom for an individual to make up his own mind, to make decisions for which he himself would be fully responsible. Read the following parable and draw your own conclusions:

"A man had two sons. He went to the first, and said, 'My boy, go and work today in the vineyard.' 'I will, sir,' the boy replied; but he never went. The father came to the second and said the same. 'I will not,' he replied, but afterward he changed his mind and went. Which of these did as his father wished? 'The second,' they said" (Matthew 21: 28–31 New English Bible).

If we study a child's nature, we find a number of qualities which are lost or muted by the time he reaches adulthood. Perhaps these ought be included in any definition we have of authentic, joyful humanity: wonder, eagerness to learn, playfulness, honesty, independence, openness to everyone. Psychiatrist R. D. Laing claims that adults do their best, by the time a youngster is 15 or so, to brainwash him of most of these qualities. Parents force him into their own image, "a half-crazed creature more or less adjusted to a mad world." Our weapon for distorting the child's childlikeness is violence masquerading as love. "Love lets the other be, but with affection and concern. Violence attempts to constrain the other's freedom, to force him to act in the way we desire, but with ultimate lack of concern, with indifference to the other's existence or destiny." *

Let us examine the qualities of childlikeness which might be related to what Jesus meant by the kingdom.

Wonder sees every experience as new, as fresh, as surprise and puzzlement. Since a child takes nothing for granted—since this is the first time he has traveled this road—he does not act automatically as most adults do, as a victim of habit. The child sees what the adult misses; his discoveries are "wonder-full." So jaded are most adults that it takes a landing on the moon to evoke the sense of wonder that a child gets from a stone, a gnarled tree, an animal, a loved person, or a simple story. These may elicit only a yawn from the average adult, instead of a pleasant surprise. In great souls like Gandhi, Einstein, and Schweitzer, even the commonplace evoked a sense of wonder. They were apostles of sensitiveness, and as such they were childlike.

A child is *eager to learn*. We have only to watch a child to see that he is hungry for new skills, that he seeks answers to puzzling phenomena. The questions "how" and "why" are frequently on his lips. We can only decry the tragedy when we see how often the curiosity, the love of learning are turned off at about the third grade by "schooling" that assumes a child must be driven to learn.

Playfulness is natural to a child who has not been hurt by life. Whether it involves make-believe, or dancing, or running, or fondling, or throwing stones, or inventing games, the child revels in the delight of using all his senses. (We are now

* R. D. Laing, *The Politics of Experience.* New York: Pantheon Books, 1967, p. 36.

discovering that a certain playfulness of mind and the willingness to make-believe are essential for brilliant, creative scientists. Piaget, the psychologist, tells us that by the time a child is 7, most of his play has been transformed into "rule-governed games," many of which (like Little League) look more like work-achievement than fun.

The *honesty* of small children is notorious; they call it as they see and feel it. They do not yet distort the truth in the name of manners or respect. The emperor really does not have a new suit of invisible clothes; he is naked.

Surprising as it may sound at first, a child is more *independent* than an adult. We think of a child as dependent because he cannot yet care for himself, but when you come right down to it, neither can an adult. An adult *appears* to be self-sufficient because he can purchase services and resources that make it possible for him to survive. But children clearly are more independent than their elders. It is the young child who tries what others might regard as "impractical." It is the child who is not afraid to speak out when he feels deeply about something, even if it is not in "good taste." The average adult, on the other hand, has exchanged his independence of thought and action for money, or power, or professional status until, at last, he has lost the vision and courage to live out his real convictions. He has become programmed for security. *Who* is dependent?

The small child is *open to everyone* who is friendly. He does not draw artificial lines that separate people from each other. Only after indoctrination does he learn to label himself and others as members of groups. Before that, people are people. "Who is it we are not supposed to like, mama?" one child asked his parents after hearing about riots in his city. A little boy brought a Negro friend home from school. "Hey, Mom, did you know Joey and me are different? He's left-handed."

"Except you become as little children, you will not enter the kingdom." What if we should accept "a child in the midst" as a symbol of what the world could be like, indeed, must be like, in order to survive and experience its true humanity? Can you think of a better image than this?

The psalmist speaks about our ultimate hope being "in the Lord." Where does that come in, you may ask. That's what we have been talking about. We are open to God when we courageously walk through the shadows of despair. It is then that we discover that those "who *wait* upon the Lord shall renew their strength; they shall mount up with wings as eagles. . . ." We are open to God when we begin to use our gifts and talents for good in the world around us. We are open to God when we go out to meet the world in relationships of mutual helpfulness, for "everyone who loves is a child of God and knows God . . . for God is love." We are open to God when we work for a world which is safe and secure for children, and when we help others and ourselves to recover that quality of childlikeness which Jesus associated with his kingdom.

We've come to the end of this book and I want to close with two thoughts. This is a good time to live. Is it not exciting to live in an era of revolution, when the old and new stand side-by-side in contrast and tension? I think we are fortunate to be alive when we can know both fear and hope; when our energies are needed to combine the achievements of the old era with the rich possibilities of the new; when we see the desire of increasing numbers of young people and adults to live freshly instead of automatically in a changing world.

This time, like all times, is a very good time if we know how to see it and what to do with it. Men and women are returning with renewed interest to the Master of life and death for a clue as to how to see it and what to do about it. Here stood a Man in the midst of every baffling contradiction and absurdity that we face, who held every pull of opposites in his own heart—the height of heaven and the depth of hell, the temptation of power and the desire to love, the freedom of trust and the bitterness of the lonely, the vitality of hope and the deadness of despair, the joy of life and the pain of death.

But look at what he made of them: a newly-heightened consciousness of life for man, a community of caring, a vision of
a new order of society, freedom from the tyranny of false
security, a new sense of God. Wouldn't it be something if he
were still alive, if we could be a part of him, in whom we really
live and move and have our being?